GERMANY 1918–1945

Paul Grey and
Rosemarie Little

This book is dedicated to Rhian and Nadine.

CAMBRIDGE UNIVERSITY PRESS
Cambridge, New York, Melbourne, Madrid, Cape Town,
Singapore, São Paulo, Delhi, Tokyo, Mexico City

Cambridge University Press
The Edinburgh Building, Cambridge CB2 8RU, UK

www.cambridge.org
Information on this title: www.cambridge.org/9780521568623

First published 1997
11th printing 2012

Printed in Dubai by Oriental Press

A catalogue record for this publication is available from the British Library

ISBN 978-0-521-56862-3 Paperback

Produced by Gecko Limited, Bicester, Oxon

Picture research by Marilyn Rawlings

ACKNOWLEDGEMENTS
We are grateful to the following for permission to reproduce photographs:
AKG London, pages 13 left, 14–15, 23, 30, 46 left, 47, 48, 51 left, 53, 55, 57 right, 59, 60, 61 and 62; Bayerische
Staatsbibliothek, pages 8 and 25; Bildarchiv Preussischer Kulturbesitz, pages 28 left, 31, 35 and 54; Deutsche
Bücherei, Leipzig, page 27; Camera Press, page 41 below right; ET Archive, pages 32 and 45; *Evening Standard /*
Solo Syndication/Centre for the Study of Cartoon and Caricature, University of Kent, Canterbury, page 50;
Hulton Getty Picture Collection, pages 26 and 36; Imperial War Museum, pages 6, 34 and 58; The Kobal
Collection, pages 28 above right (Universal) and 28 below right (Decla-Bioscope); Peter Newark's Pictures,
pages 43 and 49; Popperfoto, pages 27, 41 above right, 46 right, 62 inset and 63; Süddeutscher Verlag, pages 5,
39 and 42; Topham Picturepoint, pages 17, 20, 33, 37 below, 40, 41 above left and below left and 57 left;
Ullstein Bilderdienst, pages 9, 13 right, 37 above, 38 and 61 inset; Visual Arts Library, London/Berlin,
Nationalgalerie, page 29; Wiener Library, pages 24, 51 right and 52.

Cover illustration: a propaganda poster for the Hitler Youth, courtesy of Bundesarchiv, Koblenz

Contents

Germany and the First World War

The war began in 1914 and ended in 1918. During those four years over 10 million people were killed and millions more were wounded, gassed or uprooted from their homes. Churches, schools, factories, farmland and even whole towns had been destroyed, mostly in France. This mass destruction was partly the result of new weapons like aeroplanes, tanks and submarines. The war also had serious economic effects: it is estimated to have cost about £45,000 million.

What caused the war in August 1914?

Historians still debate the causes of the war. Most agree that an immediate or short-term cause was the assassination of Archduke Franz Ferdinand. His death in Sarajevo triggered a chain of decisions by European statesmen which ended with Britain declaring war against Germany on 4 August 1914.

However, the assassination alone does not explain what caused the war. At the time, Europe was divided into two armed camps: the Central Powers (Germany and Austria-Hungary) and the Allied Powers (Russia, France and Britain). This division created great tensions which affected the attitudes of decision-makers in the governments of these countries. A naval arms race between Britain and Germany fuelled suspicions. Governments were advised by their generals that if a conflict did start, it would all be over within a few months. In Germany, a plan was devised to defeat France in six weeks before turning east to finish off Russia. This was called the Schlieffen Plan.

What did people expect to happen?

At the outset, most British people saw the war as a wonderful opportunity to serve their 'King and Country', see off the enemy before Christmas, and return home to a hero's welcome. In Germany, Adolf Hitler's emotions were shared by thousands who greeted enthusiastically the declaration of war in Germany: 'I am not ashamed to admit that I was carried away by the enthusiasm of the moment and that I sank down on my knees to thank Heaven for allowing me to live in such a time.' There were calls for national unity: the German Kaiser (Emperor) told crowds in Berlin that he no longer recognised political parties but 'only German brothers'. These hopes and expectations were ill-founded. Quick victories were not achieved as the mud and shell-holes slowed the attacks of both sides.

	The 'Central Powers'
	Countries formerly allied with the Central Powers, but remaining neutral on the outbreak of war, and later joining the Allied Powers.
	The 'Entente' or 'Allied Powers' following the German attack on Belgium.
	Neutral states

The alliance system in Europe on 4 August 1914.

A huge crowd in the German city of Munich welcomes the news of war on 1 August 1914. Picked out in the photograph is Adolf Hitler, an unknown at the time.

The course of the war

The Schlieffen Plan, which the Germans hoped would prevent war on two fronts, failed early on. The German advance was brought to a halt by French and British troops; trenches were dug at the front-line and a stalemate developed. Attempts to break it failed. Moving forward even a mile or two cost many thousands of lives. On the first day of the Battle of the Somme in 1916, the British lost some 60,000 soldiers trying to break through German lines. Still the deadlock was not broken.

At sea there were no decisive battles. The Battle of Jutland between the British and German navies was inconclusive. Unable to wipe out the British fleet, the Germans used submarines (U-boats) to destroy British ships and cut off vital supplies. Some of the ships which were sunk came from America. Angered by these attacks, which cost the lives of innocent citizens, the USA declared war against Germany in April 1917.

As American soldiers strengthened the Allies on the Western Front, Russia was losing to Germany in the east. Very little had gone right for the Russians since the start of the war in 1914. Two revolutions in Russia in 1917 produced a new Communist government, which immediately sued for peace. The Treaty of Brest-Litovsk was signed in March 1918. Huge amounts of land and resources were handed over to Germany. But success for Germany in the east was followed by failure in the west a few months later.

WHY DID GERMANY LOSE?

> Fighting the war on two fronts, in east and west, put enormous strain on the German economy. In the last few months of the war, Germans suffered from food and fuel shortages; there were riots and mutinies. The Allies' blockade of German ports was very effective.

> The French and British were able to use resources from their empires. From the West Indies, India and African colonies came soldiers and supplies of all kinds.

> By July 1918, one million American soldiers had landed in France to bolster the Allies' efforts.

In August 1918 the Allies made a decisive breakthrough and Germany headed towards defeat.

Discussion points

> Why were so many people in favour of war in 1914?

> What problems do you think would face the peacemakers after the war?

The Treaty of Versailles: what did it decide?

The Armistice

In 1918, staring defeat in the face, the German generals shifted responsibility for running the war onto the civilian government who then asked for peace. In this way the army avoided the blame for losing.

An agreement was signed to stop the fighting at 11am on 11 November 1918. This agreement was called the Armistice. Both sides laid down their arms. Germany and Austria-Hungary (the Central Powers) were economically and militarily exhausted after their bitter struggle against the Allies (Britain, France and the USA). With a blockade strangling the ports and unrest at home, Germany was in no position to carry on fighting. The Armistice, which appeared to promise a fair peace treaty, was based upon the 'Fourteen Points' which had been put forward by the President of the United States, Woodrow Wilson.

This painting by William Orpen shows the German delegates signing the Treaty of Versailles. In the centre, on the opposite side of the table, sit Wilson, Clemenceau and Lloyd George.

The Treaty of Versailles

The leaders of the three victorious powers all had different ideas about what should be put in the peace treaty.

ATTITUDES TOWARDS THE PEACE

> **Lloyd George, the British Prime Minister,** wanted a moderate peace which would not make the Germans bitter. However, he was under pressure from the British public, who wanted to 'hang the Kaiser' and 'squeeze the German lemon until the pips squeak'.

> **Clemenceau, the French Prime Minister,** wanted revenge and compensation on behalf of the French people for all the damage done to their country. 90% of France's coal and iron industries had been seized by the Germans. Clemenceau was determined that the treaty would make it impossible for Germany to attack France ever again.

> **Wilson, the US President,** wanted a fair peace. His proposals for the treaty were called the Fourteen Points. Here are some of them:

  1. There should be no secret treaties between states.
  4. All countries should reduce their level of armaments.
  8. Alsace-Lorraine should be given back to France.
  10. The different ethnic groups in Austria-Hungary should each have their own country.
  13. An independent Poland should be created. It should have access to the sea.
  14. A League of Nations should be created to settle future disputes between countries peacefully.

After meeting for six months, a treaty was agreed and presented to the Germans at the Palace of Versailles, outside Paris. With great reluctance, the German delegation signed the Treaty of Versailles on 28 June 1919.

At the heart of the document was Article 231, which clearly stated that Germany was responsible for starting the war and for causing all the damage. The victors wanted to recover their costs and to ensure that such a war could never happen again. The Treaty of Versailles was their attempt to achieve both these aims.

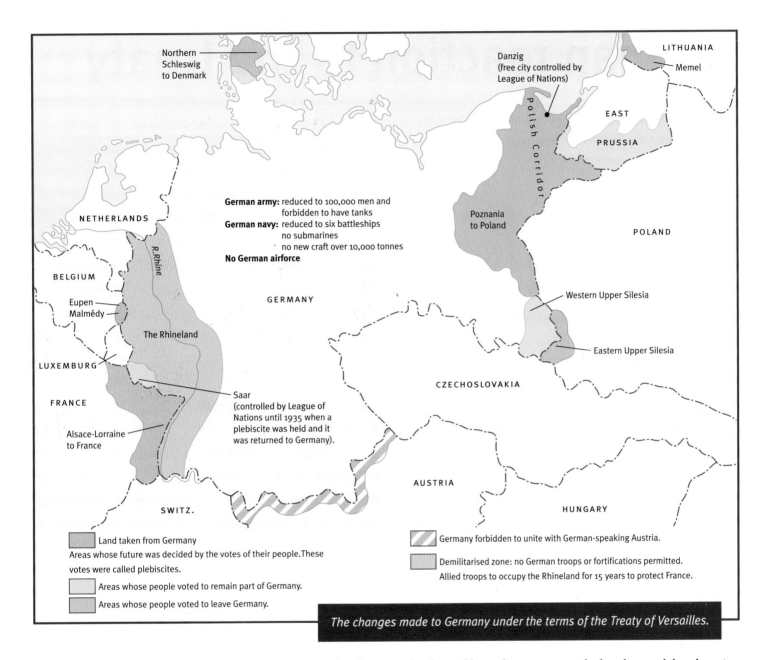

The changes made to Germany under the terms of the Treaty of Versailles.

German army: reduced to 100,000 men and forbidden to have tanks
German navy: reduced to six battleships no submarines no new craft over 10,000 tonnes
No German airforce

Northern Schleswig to Denmark

Danzig (free city controlled by League of Nations)

LITHUANIA
Memel

EAST PRUSSIA

Polish Corridor

Poznania to Poland

POLAND

NETHERLANDS

BELGIUM

Eupen Malmédy

The Rhineland

R. Rhine

GERMANY

Western Upper Silesia

Eastern Upper Silesia

LUXEMBURG

Saar (controlled by League of Nations until 1935 when a plebiscite was held and it was returned to Germany).

FRANCE

Alsace-Lorraine to France

CZECHOSLOVAKIA

AUSTRIA

HUNGARY

SWITZ.

Land taken from Germany
Areas whose future was decided by the votes of their people. These votes were called plebiscites.

Areas whose people voted to remain part of Germany.

Areas whose people voted to leave Germany.

Germany forbidden to unite with German-speaking Austria.

Demilitarised zone: no German troops or fortifications permitted. Allied troops to occupy the Rhineland for 15 years to protect France.

In addition to all the treaty provisions shown on the map, the Allies also demanded reparations from Germany in compensation for the damage caused during the war. In 1921, the total was put at £6,600 million. It was to be paid in goods and money in equal instalments until 1987. Finally, all Germany's colonies in the Far East and Africa were taken from her and were placed in the care of France and Britain in what was called the 'mandate' system.

The German public called the Treaty of Versailles the 'Diktat' or dictated peace because there was no discussion of its terms. It was certainly not the sort of peace they had pictured when the Armistice was signed. Disillusioned by the 'Diktat', ordinary Germans were easily persuaded to believe the myth of the 'stab in the back' – the rumour that German soldiers had not lost the war but could have fought on if the civilian government had not betrayed them by suing for peace. Having 'stabbed the army in the back' by signing the Armistice in November 1918, the new democratic government was excluded from the peace negotiations, and then forced to sign the Treaty of Versailles. Labelled the 'November criminals', German politicians found it very hard to destroy the myth about their role in ending the war.

Discussion points

> Which Allied leader appeared to offer the Germans the fairest treatment during discussions on the peace?

German reaction to the treaty

You have seen how the Treaty of Versailles was designed to punish Germany for starting the war and to prevent her from fighting another. From the Allies' point of view this seemed very reasonable; but how did the Germans react? Did the German government and the German public share the same view?

How did Germany react to the Treaty of Versailles?

In considering this question you should bear in mind that a year earlier, in March 1918, it was the German government who was dictating peace terms to the new Communist government in Russia. The Treaty of Brest-Litovsk was very harsh: Russia surrendered the Ukraine, Finland and their Polish and Baltic lands. Russia handed over huge resources to Germany under the terms of the treaty: 33% of her population, 32% of her farm land, 27% of her railways, 54% of her industries and 89% of her coal mines. In August 1918, the Germans went further by imposing reparations on Russia and by taking control of Livonia and Estonia. The Armistice signed in November 1918 invalidated the Treaty of Brest-Litovsk. In the following year, the Germans found themselves at the receiving end of the Versailles treaty. Germany lost 100% of her pre-war colonies, 48% of her iron production, 16% of her coal production, 13% of her territory and 12% of her population.

>> How do the two treaties compare?
   Which was harsher?

SOURCE A

A cartoon published in July 1919 in the conservative newspaper Kladderadatsch. *It was entitled 'Clemenceau the Vampire'. The figure on the bed represents Germany.*

SOURCE B

This extract is taken from a newspaper report which appeared in the New York Times *in July 1919.*

The immediate effect of the signing [*of the treaty*] was a blaze of indignation in the German press and depression among the people. In Berlin an atmosphere of profound gloom settled on the city. Several papers appeared with black borders on their Versailles articles... In Berlin on 24 June, a number of German officers and soldiers seized 15 flags which had been captured from the French in 1870 and publicly burned them... Serious mob violence was in evidence, especially in Berlin and Hamburg, throughout the week of the signing of the peace treaty.

A protest march against the Treaty of Versailles in Munich in July 1919.

A shock to the German people

The German public seem to have been unprepared for the contents of the treaty, but the German government knew what was likely to be in it. They had seen the grim mood of the Allies during the Armistice negotiations and they had not been invited to the peace discussions in Paris. They did nothing in the early months of 1919 to prepare the German people for the shock of the Versailles treaty.

SOURCE D

An extract from discussions among members of the German government about the possible terms of the peace treaty. These discussions took place on 21 March 1919.

Count Rantzau (*Foreign Minister*): Let me make a few opening comments. Our enemies will give us the completed draft of the peace treaty with the words 'Take it or leave it'. The draft treaty will look very different from President Wilson's 14 point programme. I think our discussions should focus on these issues: territorial questions; reparations questions; colonies; disarmament; and war guilt.

Landsberg (*Minister for Justice*): The questions of guilt and reparations cannot be separated. The march into Belgium by our troops in August 1914 resulted from an emergency, but was not self-defence. Emergencies do not take away our responsibility for the damages, so we should agree to making some payment but this should be small.

>> Activities

1 Study Source A. What does it tell you about German attitudes towards the Versailles treaty?

 How do Sources B and C help you assess the reliability of Source A in your investigation of German public opinion?

2 Study Sources A to C. What was public reaction to the way Germany was being treated by the Allies and how widespread was it?

3 Study Source D and use your knowledge of the Treaty of Brest-Litovsk. Were the German government and public hypocritical in their reaction to the Versailles treaty?

4 Use Sources A to D and your background knowledge to judge which of these statements is the more accurate:

 a Both government and public in Germany were unprepared for defeat in the war and the punishment set out in the Treaty of Versailles.

 b The German government knew that they would lose the war and would suffer under the peace but the public thought the opposite.

A fair treaty?

Historians have argued about the Treaty of Versailles ever since 1919. Their interpretations of the treaty have changed over time: not all historians arrive at the same judgement nor do they share the views of people commenting in 1919.

How have historians interpreted the Treaty of Versailles?

The 1920s

During the 1920s, historians tended to judge the peacemakers of 1919 very favourably. There was, however, a growing realisation that Germany needed to recover so that trade could flourish; it was generally agreed that the reparations bill was far too high. The amount was cut in 1924 and again in 1929. A healthier German economy was welcomed and European security and peace were still intact because the other elements of the treaty were being enforced. German leaders were working towards making Germany respectable again in the family of nations.

SOURCE A

From The World Crisis *written by Winston Churchill (British) in 1929.*

... a fair judgement upon the Versailles treaty is that the wishes of the various populations were met. Probably less than 3% of the European population are now living under governments whose nationality they reject. No solution could have been free from hardship and the odd mistake.

The restriction on armaments enforced on Germany is today considered to be something which all nations should aim for. The unfair economic punishments of the Versailles treaty have already been swept away.

The 1930s and 1940s

During the 1930s and 1940s, historians' views on the treaty were affected by the times they lived in. Hitler had come to power in 1933 and set about destroying the Versailles agreement by re-occupying the Rhineland in 1936, invading Austria in 1938, rearming all the while. War broke out in 1939 after Britain and France stopped appeasing Hitler. After six years of fighting and 50 million deaths, the war ended in 1945.

A map of central and eastern Europe showing the boundary changes made by the Paris peace settlement.

SOURCE B

From The Carthaginian Peace *written by Etienne Mantoux (French) in 1945.*

The amount of reparations Germany had to pay was not that much. In the six years before the outbreak of war in 1939 Hitler had spent seven times as much money on rearming Germany as the country would have paid in reparations.

The worst part of the peace treaty lay in the boundary changes to central and south-eastern Europe. A strong Germany was left surrounded by a string of small states who had to rely for their security on countries very far away.

More recent interpretations

One result of the 1939–45 conflict was that the Cold War created tension between capitalist and communist countries. Germany itself was split in two until it was reunified in December 1990. Once more, the questions historians ask and the judgements they make reflect the times they live in.

SOURCE C

From The Weimar Republic *written by Eberhard Kolb (German) in 1988.*

It has been said that the Treaty of Versailles, depending on one's point of view, was either too severe or too lenient. In forming a historical judgement today it is important to recognise two points. Firstly, the treaty was a heavy burden for a young democracy, and the Allies did not act wisely in being so harsh on those German politicians and political parties who shared President Wilson's ideas concerning international co-operation and friendship...

Secondly, despite the Treaty of Versailles, Germany was still a great power with the opportunity in the long term of again playing a part in European affairs and with greater freedom than she had had in 1914. The Treaty of Versailles actually strengthened Germany rather than weakened her. The reason for this was that Communist Russia had been dislodged from Central Europe and for a long time was absorbed in her internal problems. If Germany had pursued a steady and cautious policy towards south-eastern Europe, that area might have been turned into an area of German influence.

>> Activities

Study all the sources and use your background knowledge.

1 How have historians' interpretations of the Versailles treaty changed over time? Can you suggest any reasons for this?

2 'Historians' interpretations of the evidence about the Treaty of Versailles have been influenced by their nationality.' How far do you agree with this statement in the context of this enquiry?

3 'Contemporaries saw the treaty as a harsh punishment, but today some historians view it as a missed opportunity for Germany to become stronger.' How do you explain this contradiction?

4 What have you learned from this investigation about how and why interpretations of the past change and develop?

The Weimar Republic

War and revolution

In 1918 Germany began to crack under the strain of war. Shortages, power cuts, inflation and anti-war demonstrations were bad enough, but then a lethal virus swept across Europe: influenza. Thousands of soldiers and civilians died. With the German army in disorder, General Ludendorff announced in the Reichstag (the German parliament) that Germany was in grave danger of defeat. A peace must be made soon before Germany lost on the battlefield.

President Wilson offered an armistice on condition that Germany became more democratic. In particular, he wanted the Reichstag to have greater power and the Kaiser to have less. At first the Kaiser would not budge. Then, on 28 October 1918, sailors at Kiel refused to put to sea to fight the British. From this point on, Germany descended into chaos. The government in Berlin lost control and could not stop the ordinary civilians and soldiers seizing power. Between 4 and 6 November, mutineers seized control of the ports of Rostock, Cuxhaven and Lübeck. Revolution then spread inland. In Saxony and Bavaria, socialists established republics. Lacking the support of his army generals, the Kaiser fled to Holland on 10 November, never to return again. In his place came not a hereditary monarch or emperor but an elected politician: Friedrich Ebert, leader of the Social Democratic Party.

The new democratic Germany

After the Armistice had been signed, Friedrich Ebert had two tasks: to hold democratic elections so a new government could be formed and to hammer out a new constitution detailing how the German people would be ruled. Elections in January 1919 did not produce a clear winner. The Social Democratic Party gained the most seats but had to join up with two other parties in order to form a government with a majority in the new parliament. Coalition governments were to be a feature right through the period 1918–30.

Politicians decided that Berlin was not a calm enough place in which to settle the details of the new constitution so they met in a small town called Weimar. Within six months the constitution was ready. Germany was, at least on paper, a democracy like Britain, France or the United States.

Period of crisis, 1918–23

During this five-year period, the newly formed Weimar Republic survived some serious crises. From both the left and the right came putsches (revolts), assassinations and anti-government propaganda. The economy, already weakened by the war effort, was further damaged by demands for reparations from the Allies and by terrifying inflation. And always the Weimar governments were baited about the 'stab in the back' and the punishing Treaty of Versailles which they had signed.

INFLATION

The price of bread in Berlin in German marks.

1918	0.54	1923	January	250.00
1921	3.90		June	3,465.00
1922	163.50		September	1,512,000.00
			November	201,000,000,000.00

ECONOMIC PROBLEMS

> 1918   2.4 million Germans killed. 70% of the cost of the war met by loans.

> 1921   Government prints more money to pay for the reparations.

> 1923   Government prints more money to pay the wages of workers on strike in the Ruhr.

ATTEMPTS TO TAKE POWER

> 1919 (January): the Spartacist revolt. A group of Communists tried to take control of Berlin. Ex-soldiers, the Freikorps, were let loose and killed the leaders.

> 1920 (March): the Kapp Putsch. Wolfgang Kapp led the Freikorps in an attempt to take control of Berlin. The workers came out on strike, bringing the city to a standstill. Kapp was arrested.

> 1923 (November): the Beer Hall Putsch (or Munich Putsch). Adolf Hitler, with the support of some leading army figures, tried to take over Munich. The police and army restored control. The leaders were arrested and put on trial for treason.

IMPLEMENTATION OF THE TREATY OF VERSAILLES

> 1919 French, British and US troops move into the Rhineland.

> 1920 The peace treaty comes into force.

> 1921 Reparations total decided: £6,600 million.

> 1922 (December) Germany defaults on her reparation payments.

> 1923 (January) French and Belgian troops enter the Ruhr to take goods from Germany to maintain reparation payments. The German workers come out on strike and refuse to co-operate with the French.

> 1923 (September) Stresemann calls off passive resistance in the Ruhr.

> 1923 (November) New currency introduced: the Rentenmark.

A French soldier guarding a train full of German coal from the Ruhr. In 1923, the French invaded to take goods back to France for reparation payment.

Period of recovery, 1924–29

What brought stability and recovery to Germany was a huge loan from the United States in an agreement called the Dawes Plan. This £40 million loan, combined with a new currency to replace the one so devalued by inflation, revived the German economy. Much of this short-term loan was used by the government on housing and public works. Unemployment figures fell. Prosperity was further enhanced when reparations were cut as part of the Dawes Plan and cut again by the Young Plan in 1929. Germans were finally enjoying good times, and support for politicians on the extreme left and right who wanted radical change dwindled away at election time.

good guys USA

One politician who was popular during this period was Gustav Stresemann, the German Foreign Minister. He combined stability on the domestic front with success abroad. In 1925 Germany signed the Locarno treaty. The next year she was allowed to join other countries on an equal footing at the League of Nations. *good!* Germany signed the Kellogg–Briand Pact in 1928. These two agreements marked Germany's reintegration into the family of European powers. The following year Britain and France agreed to withdraw their troops from the Rhineland, five years ahead of the schedule laid down by the Treaty of Versailles. *things are looking up!*

In 1928, the Weimar Republic was celebrating its tenth birthday. The young democracy had weathered many storms and Germany was once more respected abroad. Nothing, it seemed, could spoil Stresemann's apparent success and Germany's revival since the years of crisis. *ummmm... Hitler*

Gustav Stresemann.

Discussion points

> Why do wars sometimes bring about revolutions like the one in Germany in 1918?

> In which year was the existence of the Weimar Republic most in danger?

The Spartacist revolt

Historians do not only describe events, they interpret them. One label they often use is 'revolution'. Is this a justifiable interpretation of events in Germany in 1918–19?

Was there a revolution in 1918–19?

The chaos in Germany in 1918 saw the power of central government in Berlin break down as Workers' and Soldiers' Councils took control in most towns and cities. The rulers were no longer trusted and ordinary people were enjoying the taste of power. Then the Kaiser abdicated and a republic was declared in Berlin by Ebert, the leader of the Social Democratic Party (SPD), the moderate socialists. In December 1918, a national congress of Councils met in Berlin. Since most of the delegates were moderate socialists, they supported Ebert's proposal to hold elections for a National Assembly. But the revolutionary socialists (Spartacists) disagreed: an election would mean that upper-class and middle-class Germans would still run Germany and the workers would lose out.

The Spartacists refused to let their chance of creating a socialist Germany slip away. In January 1919, Karl Liebknecht and Rosa Luxemburg led an armed uprising in Berlin to snatch power from Ebert. From Ebert's point of view, Germany needed law and order more

[handwritten: wanted socialism and fair representation]

>> Activities   *[handwritten: Ebert crushed them]*

1   Look up the word 'revolution' in a dictionary. Do the events in Germany in 1918–19 deserve the label 'revolution'? If so, why?

2   Compare developments in Germany with other events which historians call revolutions. For example, what similarities and differences are there with the Russian revolutions in 1917?

3   One historian has labelled developments in Germany in 1918–19 a 'half-finished revolution'. How far do you agree with this interpretation?

than it needed socialism. He could not rely on the army because it had dissolved after the Armistice so instead he used the Freikorps, bands of ex-servicemen who hated socialism in any shape or form. Brutally, they crushed the Berlin revolt. Liebknecht and Luxemburg were murdered. The surviving Spartacists saw this as treachery: the moderate socialists had betrayed the working class. This split on the left was to prove very costly. When German democracy started to crumble after 1930, the workers were unable to unite in order to save it.

SOURCE A

Demands made by the Spartacists on 7 October 1918.

The struggle for real democracy is not about a National Assembly and the vote; it is concerned with the real enemies of working people: private property, control over the army and justice. We demand the transfer of power to Workers' and Soldiers' Councils; the nationalisation of all property, and the reorganisation of the army so that ordinary soldiers have power.

SOURCE B

From a speech by Max Cohen, a member of the SPD, the moderate socialist party led by President Ebert.

The will of the people can only be reflected in a National Assembly elected by every German. The Workers' and Soldiers' Councils can only express the will of some of the people not all of them.

Ebert used force to crush the Spartacist revolt because he was so scared of Germany collapsing into chaos. This had happened in Russia after the 1917 socialist revolution. His fear prevented him from supporting the Workers' Councils. If he had worked with them, together they could have introduced democratic reforms in the civil service, the army and the judiciary. As it was, the 'old guard' survived; only the Kaiser himself was swept away.

Freikorps use bales of paper as a barricade during fighting outside newspaper offices in Berlin, 1919.

Democracy in Weimar Germany

In August 1919 the new republic adopted a new constitution so that the country could be run as a democracy.

How democratic was the Weimar Republic?

The parliament

[handwritten: new parliament]

A new parliament (Reichstag) was established with members elected by Germans over the age of 20. Voting took place in secret and the number of seats a political party won in the Reichstag was dependent upon the proportion of votes cast. Called 'proportional representation', this system never produced a majority of seats for any one party; coalitions had to be formed. *[handwritten: similar to MoR]*

The President

A President was elected separately so that he could act as a check on the Reichstag's power. He held office for seven years. His *[handwritten: term]* powers included the ability to appoint and dismiss the government. He could dissolve the Reichstag and, under Article 48, he could *[handwritten: Syria + Egypt]* announce a 'state of emergency' to preserve law and order in a crisis. Under these circumstances he could assume enormous power by setting aside the Fundamental Rights (a series of articles focusing on the rights of the individual). *[handwritten: scary]*

SOURCE A

The main features of the pre-1919 German constitution.

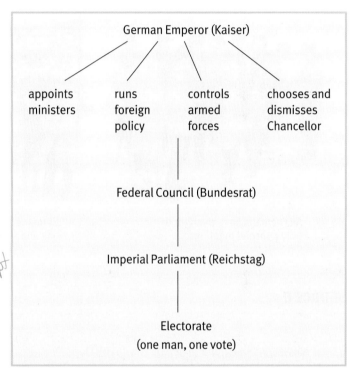

Federal government

The Weimar constitution established a federal system of government. This means that the power to make and enforce laws was shared between the central government in Berlin and the 18 state (Länder) governments. For example, Berlin had control over taxation and religion; the Länder governments had control over the police, courts and schools.

In addition to these provisions on the running of government, there were 56 articles setting out the rights of individual Germans.

SOURCE B

Personal freedom is guaranteed. No-one can be arrested unless they have broken the law.

The home of every German is a place of safety for him. The authorities cannot enter it without proper cause.

Every German has the right to express his opinion freely by word, writing, printed matter or picture.

All Germans have the right to hold peaceful meetings.

All Germans have the right to form unions and societies.

Property is guaranteed.

Some of the 56 articles and Fundamental Rights in the Weimar constitution of 1919.

SOURCE C

This map shows most of the 18 German Länder in 1919 after the Treaty of Versailles.

>> Activities

1 Describe the differences between the pre-1919 constitution (Source A) and the new Weimar constitution.

2 Use the background information and all the Sources. Can you see any potential dangers for German democracy within the new constitution?

Opposition to Weimar Germany: part one

You have seen how the new constitution seemed to provide Germans with a democratic framework for conducting politics. However, democracy needs to have deep roots in society and the support of many people if it is to survive. The Weimar Republic faced opposition from many groups in German society.

Who opposed the Weimar Republic and why?

The democratic politicians of the new republic failed to take the opportunity presented to them by the 1918 revolution to remove from power those people who opposed the new system. The army, the police, the judiciary, the schools and the universities were all staffed by people who disliked, even hated, the democratic system. Many looked back longingly to the days before 1914 when the Kaiser was the unquestioned ruler and Germany was a first-rate power with an empire and a strong, growing economy. In those days, there was a feeling of certainty about living in Germany. Now, during the 1920s, there seemed to be nothing but uncertainty.

Even some politicians and their parties did not support the Weimar Republic. Although they took part in elections, they despised the democratic process. One such party was formed by Anton Drexler in 1919. It was called the German Workers' Party. Drexler was soon replaced as leader by Adolf Hitler, who renamed it the National Socialist German Workers' Party, or Nazi Party for short.

In this two-part investigation you will study evidence which will help you to understand the attitudes and beliefs of Germans who opposed Weimar democracy. The second part of the investigation looks specifically at the ideas and policies of the new Nazi Party.

Understanding attitudes and beliefs

During the 1920s the enemies of the Weimar Republic were very critical of the lack of 'strong' government. In some ways they were right: every single Weimar government was a coalition – usually an alliance of three political parties. These parties did not always agree; squabbling broke out and often coalitions broke up and new ones formed. The parties which featured most frequently in coalitions during the 1920s were the SPD (Social Democratic Party), the Centre Party and the DDP (German Democratic Party). Other political parties campaigned actively against the Republic. Even so, at election time, most Germans voted for parties which supported the Weimar democratic system.

Vote Communist! An election poster of the KPD shows the ghost of the murdered Communist, Karl Liebknecht, threatening his enemies.

SOURCE A

The main political parties in the Reichstag including those which formed the coalition governments during the 1920s. The parties are displayed left to right on the political spectrum.

PARTY	KPD (Communist Party, previously the Spartacists)	SPD (Social Democratic Party)	DDP (German Democratic Party)
SUPPORT	the working class	mostly from the industrial working class and some lower middle class	mostly middle class
POLICIES	against the Republic and in favour of a workers' revolution like the Russian model	supported the Republic; wanted social reforms to help working people and the less well-off	supported the Republ strong belief in individual freedom

SOURCE B

Percentage of the total vote won by the main parties in elections between 1919 and 1928.

	1919	1920	1924 May	1924 Dec	1928
Communists	—	2	12	9	11
Social Democratic Party	38	21	21	26	30
German Democratic Party	19	8	6	6	5
Centre Party	20	18	17	18	15
German People's Party	4	14	9	10	9
German Nationalist Party	10	15	19	21	14
Nazis	—	—	7	3	2
Minor Parties	9	22	9	7	14

SOURCE C

Growth of industrial production in Germany between 1880 and 1930.

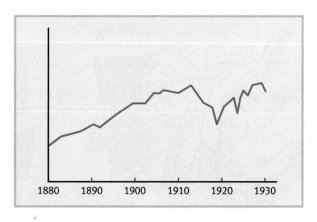

SOURCE D

From an interview with an officer of the Freikorps in 1919.

It really turned the stomachs of us old soldiers to see how quickly they got rid of the black-white-red flag of the old Empire. Under this flag thousands of soldiers lie buried in enemy territory. I don't hide the fact that I'm a monarchist. When you've served your Emperor for 30 years you can't just say: from tomorrow I'm a republican.

SOURCE E

This extract is taken from a report in a right-wing newspaper, Oletzkoer Zeitung, *in August 1921. It comments on the assassination of Matthias Erzberger, a government minister and member of the Centre Party.*

Erzberger, the man who is alone responsible for the humiliating armistice; Erzberger, the man who is responsible for the Versailles 'treaty of shame'; Erzberger has at last received the punishment suitable for a traitor.

Justice?

Judges were supposed to uphold the democratic laws in Germany fairly and justly. However, many of them gave lenient punishments to right-wingers who had committed violent political crimes while left-wingers were given harsh penalties. A communist called the Weimar state a 'robber's republic' and was sent to prison for four weeks. A right-winger who called it a 'Jews' republic' was only fined 70 marks.

Centre Party	DVP (German People's Party)	DNVP (German Nationalist Party)	NSDAP (National Socialist German Workers' Party, Nazi Party)
Roman Catholics from all classes	the wealthy middle class, especially the owners of businesses; led by Gustav Stresemann	middle and upper classes including some government officials and soldiers	nationalists and conservatives on the right of German politics including some Freikorps and lower middle-class people
supported the Republic and the interests of the Roman Catholic Church	really monarchists; came to accept the Republic with great reluctance; wanted government to support trade and industry	against the Republic; strongly nationalist; wanted strong central government to make Germany strong and powerful again	against the Republic; in favour of strong government

SOURCE F

This cartoon was published in 1929, the year of Stresemann's death, in a German newspaper, Vorwärts. The nurse is saying 'You're too late, Stresemann is dead'. The Nazis following Hugenberg are carrying a stink bomb, a bucket of manure and posters saying 'Traitor' and 'Stresemann, rot in hell'. (Hugenberg became leader of the DNVP in 1928.)

SOURCE G

Political murders in Germany between 1919 and 1923.

	Murders by the extreme left	Murders by the extreme right
Number of murders	22	354
Number of murderers sentenced by the courts	38	24
Average length of prison sentence	15 years	4 months
Number of murderers executed	10	0

>> Activities

1 Study Sources A and B. Which political parties did not completely support the Weimar Republic? How much electoral support did these parties have during the 1920s?

2 Study Sources C, D and E. How would the author of Source D use evidence from Sources C and E to criticise the Weimar Republic?

3 Study Sources E and F. What do these Sources tell you about attitudes towards

   a Weimar democracy

   b Erzberger and Stresemann?

4 Use all the Sources and what you have learned so far about the Weimar Republic. Which groups of Germans appear not to have supported the Weimar Republic and what were the reasons for their opposition?

Opposition to Weimar Germany: part two

As you saw in the previous investigation, opposition to Weimar democracy came from many quarters. Some of Weimar's bitterest enemies were ex-soldiers, those who had fought and survived the Great War but came home to find revolution and their army careers ruined by the Treaty of Versailles. One of those most bitter about the defeat was a young army corporal named Adolf Hitler.

What were the ideas and policies of the Nazi Party?

Hitler was born in Braunau in Austria in 1889. Success at secondary school soon turned sour when he went to Vienna hoping to attend art school. Twice he applied for a place and twice he was rejected. His dreams of becoming a painter were shattered. For a few years he became a homeless drifter making a little money from his paintings. Then, when war broke out in 1914, Hitler's desperate years came to an end. His life took on new purpose. He went to Germany to join up and to contribute to a glorious victory — or so he thought.

As the war ended in 1918 so did Hitler's most 'unforgettable' experience as a corporal in the German army. He was twice rewarded for bravery with the Iron Cross. He had lived and breathed the team spirit of the trenches, seen Germans unite against a common enemy and sacrifice their lives for the Fatherland. Now that the war was over, what was he to do?

Hitler and the Nazi Party

In Munich, Hitler soon found work as a routine surveillance officer for the army. Many nationalist and racist groups had formed immediately after the war and Hitler was employed to spy on one of them: the German Workers' Party. Anton Drexler, the founder of the party, was so impressed by Hitler that in September 1919 he invited him to join the group as its fifty-fifth member and to become responsible for recruitment and propaganda. The ex-corporal relished the post. Hitler was such a good speaker at meetings that he

SOURCE A

This Nazi poster shows a worker smashing 'International High Finance' in the name of socialism. On other occasions, the Nazis stressed the 'national' elements of their programme to appeal to the business classes.

was chosen to launch the German Workers' Party programme on 24 February 1920. It contained 25 points and was partly written and edited by Hitler. He told his audience that the programme was 'unchangeable'. In the same speech, the new party name was announced: from now on it would be known as the National Socialist German Workers' Party or Nazi Party for short. (The term 'Nazi' is a shortened version of the German word 'nationalsozialistisch' meaning national socialist.)

SOURCE B

Extracts from the Nazi Party programme (1920).

1 We demand the union of all Germans into a greater Germany.

2 We demand that Germany be treated in the same way as other countries and we demand the annulling of the Treaty of Versailles.

3 We demand land for our growing population.

4 Only a fellow German can have right of citizenship. A fellow German can only be so if he is of German parentage. This excludes Jews.

6 Only German citizens shall have the right to vote; and they alone shall hold public office.

8 All immigration of non-Germans must stop immediately.

14 We demand that large industries share their profits with the workers.

15 We demand generous improvements in the old age pension system.

17 We demand a new law which would allow property to be confiscated without compensation if this is in the general interest of the nation.

24 We demand the freedom of religion in Germany so long as religion does not endanger the position of the state or the moral standards of the German race. The party opposes the Jewish religion for its love of wealth.

25 In order to achieve this programme, the party demands the setting up of a strong central government with complete authority for parliament over the whole country.

Later in the 1920s, Hitler amended point 17 of the Nazi Party programme which had allowed for the confiscation of certain private property without compensation. To woo middle-class voters, Hitler now said that the Party would only confiscate property owned by Jews.

SOURCE C

The Nazi Party flag.

SOURCE D

An extract from Mein Kampf *written by Adolf Hitler in 1924.*

As National Socialists we see our programme in our flag. In the red we see the social idea of the movement, in the white we see the nationalistic idea, and in the swastika we see our mission to achieve the victory of Aryan man.

Discussion point

> Which of the three colours in the Nazi Party flag received most attention in the 1920 programme?

Even at this early stage, membership of the Nazi Party was spread across all classes of Germans. Most members were lower middle class – shopkeepers and small businessmen, for example. It was they who set the tone of the organisation and its meetings: male-dominated, beer-swilling, authoritarian, anti-semitic and anti-intellectual. There were some members from the working class: craftworkers were particularly attracted to the Party. Some from the elite of German society also swelled Hitler's movement: managers, academics and university students.

>> Activities

Study Sources A, B, C and D.

1 Make a list of those Nazi policies which were 'nationalist' and those which were 'socialist'.

2 When he announced the Nazi Party programme in 1920, Hitler said it was 'unchangeable', yet later in the 1920s he did amend it. Does this mean that Source B is unreliable and cannot be used to investigate Hitler's attitudes and beliefs in the 1920s?

3 Why do you think the lower middle class were particularly attracted by Hitler, his policies and his movement?

1924–29: stabilisation and recovery?

Until recently the general picture of Germany in the period 1924–29 was one of stability and prosperity following the crises of 1918–23. With Gustav Stresemann as Chancellor in 1923 and as Foreign Minister between 1923 and 1929, the Weimar Republic recovered from its bad start. However, recent research in German archives has prompted a review of this interpretation.

To what extent did the Weimar Republic recover after 1923?

To begin with, the performance of the economy during this period has come in for close scrutiny. Some historians have pointed out that even though Germany recovered after 1923, her share of the world's industrial production between 1926 and 1929 was only 11.6% compared with 14.3% in 1913. This seems to throw doubt on the traditional picture historians have given of Germany between 1924 and 1929. Just how strong was this recovery in Germany? Did the loans from the Dawes Plan simply paper over cracks which would reappear later?

When Stresemann died through overwork in October 1929, it seemed to contemporaries that he had pulled Weimar democracy through its worst crises.

SOURCE A

An extract from Stresemann's obituary in The Times, *a British newspaper, 4 October 1929.*

By the death of Stresemann, Germany has lost her ablest statesman. He worked hard to rebuild his shattered country and for peace and co-operation abroad. In 1923 the French were in the Ruhr, the currency had collapsed, the reparations issue was unsolved. Germany seemed to be in ruins. Then he took over and under his leadership Germany is now orderly and prospering at home; in the affairs of Europe she has an important place.

THE TREATY OF LOCARNO

This treaty, signed by Stresemann in December 1925, helped restore Germany's pride. In spite of continuing problems over reparations payments, France and Britain began treating Germany less as a defeated enemy and more as an equal. Germany, France and Belgium agreed to maintain their western frontiers and to refrain from using force to alter them. Britain and Italy guaranteed the treaty.

Part of this debate depends upon how you interpret the word 'recovery'. Did Germany 'recover' its place in Europe as a respected nation and equal partner? Or did the economy 'recover' from its wartime dislocation, hyper-inflation and the burden of reparations?

SOURCE B

From A History of Germany, 1815–1945, *by William Carr, published in 1979.*

Gustav Stresemann contributed greatly to the stabilisation of the Weimar Republic. He was working for the speedy withdrawal of all foreign troops from German soil, for the removal of the moral shame of the war-guilt clause and for Germany's entry into the League of Nations.

By 1930, Germany was once again one of the world's great industrial nations. Her spectacular recovery was made possible by a huge amount of American investment; between 1924 and 1929, 25,000 million marks poured into Germany. By 1929 iron and steel, coal, chemicals and electrical products had all matched or beaten the 1913 production figures.

Up-to-date management techniques and more efficient methods of production brought about a tremendous increase in productivity; blast-furnaces, for example, trebled their output.

However, a number of scholars have found that the prosperity described by William Carr in Source B was neither secure nor widespread.

SOURCE C

This photo was taken during the negotiation of the Locarno Treaty in December 1925. From left to right: Gustav Stresemann, Sir Joseph Austen Chamberlain (Britain) and Aristide Briand (France).

SOURCE D

Table 1 shows the level of industrial production in Germany during the 1920s.

Table 2 shows the number of unemployed during the 1920s.

Table 1 *(1928 = 100)*

Year	Capital goods	Consumer goods
1920	56	51
1921	65	69
1922	70	74
1923	43	57
1924	65	81
1925	80	85
1926	77	80
1927	97	103
1928	100	100
1929	102	97
1930	84	91

Capital goods are machines used for making other goods. Consumer goods are things bought by consumers (i.e. finished products).
1928 = 100: this figure means that the standard against which all other years are measured is 100. Anything below 100 means worse, anything above means better.

Table 2

Year	No. (000s)	% of working population
1921	346	1.8
1922	215	1.1
1923	818	4.1
1924	927	4.9
1925	682	3.4
1926	2025	10.0 *good stuff!*
1927	1312	6.2
1928	1391	6.3
1929	1899	8.5
1930	3076	14.0 *not good*

SOURCE E

From Hitler and Nazism *by Dick Geary, published in 1993.*

Germany's recovery had become dependent upon foreign loans. This meant that the country was very vulnerable to movements on the money markets and the level of confidence of overseas investors.

Agricultural prices which had been steady after the early 1920s were already falling by 1927 [...] The result was a debt crisis for farmers. Nor was everything rosy in the industrial sector in the mid-20s. Heavy industry (coal, iron and steel) was already experiencing problems making profits and even in the relatively prosperous year of 1927, German steel mills worked at no more than 70% of their capacity.

good times!

>> Activities

1 Using evidence drawn from the Sources in this investigation and your knowledge from previous chapters of this book, write two accounts of the Weimar Republic, 1924–29.

   > Account **a** should explain how the period was one of stability, success and prosperity.

   > Account **b** should explain how the period was one of instability, failure and severe economic problems.

2 Two recent historians have called this period: 'deceptive stability' and 'relative stability'. Why do you think these labels have been used? What use would these two historians make of the statistics in Source D?

The Nazi Party in the 1920s

Political power can be seized in many different ways. In Germany in the 1920s, those who wanted to take control did not all share the same ideas and values. Some were in favour of using violence, others wanted to use only democratic procedures.

Why did the Nazi Party have little real success before 1930?

To answer this question, this investigation looks at two issues:

> What tactics did the Nazis use to try and gain power?

> Why did they fail?

Using violence

In the years leading up to 1924, Hitler was convinced that using violence was the only way the Nazis would gain power. What he needed was his own private army. In 1921 he established the Sturmabteilung (SA) or Stormtroopers. Many of them were ex-soldiers but there were also younger men who felt they had missed out on the war. The SA was to be the 'battering ram' of the Nazi movement.

In November 1923 the timing seemed right to seize control in Munich, the capital of Bavaria. Inflation was out of control; the French were occupying the industrial Ruhr area to collect unpaid reparations; and Gustav Stresemann had called off passive resistance by German workers which had stopped production of coal and iron in the Ruhr. The government in Berlin appeared feeble.

Hitler's plan depended upon elements of the army betraying the government and coming over to his side. Only with military support could his strategy of force be successful.

Since the beginning of the Weimar Republic, Bavaria had been a hotbed of reactionary opposition. Many right-wing groups were openly hostile to democracy. The Bavarian government also opposed Berlin and its attempts to interfere in Bavarian affairs.

On the night of 8 November 1923, Gustav von Kahr, a member of the Bavarian government, went to a political meeting at a beer hall in Munich. He was to be the main speaker. Also attending were General von Lossow, who was in command of the army in Bavaria,

SOURCE A

A cartoon drawn at the end of Hitler's trial. It shows Ludendorff and Hitler shouting from Munich beer mugs that they are Germany's saviours. The judge below says 'Rubbish! The worst charge we can bring is breaking public entertainment by-laws!'

and Colonel von Seisser, head of the state police force. Some of Hitler's SA were present in the audience with concealed weapons.

Hitler's plan was to seize Lossow, Kahr and Seisser, persuade them to join the Nazis in sparking off a national uprising against the Berlin government, and to replace democracy with strong central government. Hitler's plan failed. He entered the beer hall, rounded up Kahr, Lossow and Seisser and tried to persuade them of his plan. At first they rejected it. Then, when Hitler told them that General Ludendorff was supporting the Nazis, they changed their minds. Ludendorff arrived at the scene to lend his support.

SOURCE B

There is some doubt as to how sincere Kahr and Lossow were in their support for Hitler. As soon as they left the beer hall they raised the alarm. The state police and army were put on alert. If Hitler was to succeed, he needed military support. It was not forthcoming. A march through the streets of Munich by Hitler and his supporters the following morning attracted much public support but a police cordon brought the Nazis to a halt. A shot was fired and a police officer killed. Mayhem ensued. Soon, 16 Nazis lay dead. Hitler was arrested shortly afterwards.

Found guilty of treason, Hitler was sentenced to five years. While in prison he wrote his autobiography called *Mein Kampf* (My Struggle). He dedicated it to the 16 men who had died on 9 November 1923.

SOURCE C

This is part of the evidence which Hitler gave at his trial. Kahr, Lossow and Seisser were chief witnesses for the prosecution.

If our putsch was high treason then Lossow, Kahr and Seisser must have been committing high treason along with us, for during all these weeks we talked of nothing but the aims of which we now stand accused.

I alone bear the responsibility for the putsch but I am not a criminal because of that. There is no such thing as high treason against the traitors of 1918. I only wanted what's best for the German people.

SOURCE D

This map of Germany shows the city of Munich and the state of Bavaria.

This cartoon appeared in the magazine Simplicissimus *on 17 March 1924. It shows Hitler sitting on the shoulders of von Lossow, who is in turn sitting on the shoulders of von Kahr. Hitler is setting light to the roof of the building but von Kahr calls out to a policeman, 'Officer, arrest that arsonist up there!'*

A change of strategy

SOURCE E

This is part of a conversation which took place between Kurt Ludecke and Adolf Hitler at Landsberg Castle in 1924. Hitler is speaking to Ludecke, who supports his aims.

When I resume active work, it will be necessary to pursue a new policy. Instead of working to achieve power by an armed coup, we will have to hold our noses and enter the Reichstag against Catholic and Communist members. If outvoting them takes longer than outshooting them, at least the result will be guaranteed by their own constitution. Sooner or later we shall have a majority and after that – Germany.

>> Activities

1 Use Sources A to D.

> To what extent do the cartoonists share the same attitude towards the putsch and Hitler?

> How would you find out if these cartoons were typical of German public opinion at the time?

> Which of the cartoons is most sympathetic to Hitler's view of the trial as expressed in Source C?

2 Use Source E. In what way did the failed putsch of 1923 alter Hitler's strategy to gain political power?

THE MUNICH PUTSCH: A TURNING POINT

Later in his life, Hitler was to call his failed putsch a turning point in his political career.

> His trial was headline news in the national press.

> He was able to defeat his rivals for the leadership of the Nazi Party by pointing out that it was he and not they who had shown strength and resolve in trying to take power by force.

> Finally, the Munich putsch enabled Hitler to pursue a democratic route to power and to take the party along with him because he had demonstrated to them that violence did not work as a strategy.

1924–29: success and failure

In December 1924, Hitler was released from Landsberg prison after serving only nine months of his five-year sentence. In his absence, the Nazi Party had split into various different factions. It was officially banned and so was its paper, the *Völkischer Beobachter* (German People's Observer). What was Hitler to do now?

For Hitler and the Nazi Party, the years 1924 to 1929 brought a mixture of success and failure. At election time the Nazis failed to make much impression on the voters, but the party gradually became better organised and Hitler's personal grip on its members tightened.

DEVELOPMENTS IN THE NAZI PARTY, 1924–29

1924: Brown shirts became the official Nazi Party uniform. The swastika was adopted as the party emblem. The Stormtroopers (SA) continued to recruit.

1925: In February, the ban on the Nazis was lifted. Hitler relaunched the party.

1926: Nazi organisations were established to try to appeal to certain interest groups: the Nazi Students' League, Teachers' League, Law Officers' League and Women's League. A Nazi Party rally was held at Weimar; this began the pattern of military-style parades.

In February, Hitler defeated Gregor Strasser in a party leadership contest.

1927: Membership stood at 108,000 compared with 27,000 in 1925. Hitler reorganised the party to make it more efficient. He created a national headquarters in Munich. He insisted on central control of finance and of admission to membership.

SOURCE F

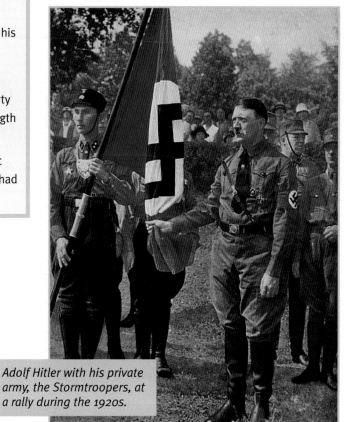

Adolf Hitler with his private army, the Stormtroopers, at a rally during the 1920s.

In spite of these developments between 1924 and 1929, the Nazi Party performed badly at elections. In May 1924 they won 32 seats in the Reichstag; in December of the same year they won 14; and in May 1928 they captured only 12. Voters were not interested in Hitler's programme. Good times had returned to Germany thanks to the Dawes Plan of 1924. The moderate parties survived the crises of 1918–23 and seemed to be handling the recovery well. Weimar democracy appeared to be working: the necessities of life – food, clothing and housing – were in more plentiful supply, and most Germans had jobs. Hitler's policies seemed out of place and rather reckless to nearly all voters.

>> Activity

Use all the Sources and your knowledge of Germany's recovery after 1923.

Even though Hitler failed to seize power in 1923 he later called the Munich putsch a turning point in his career. Can you explain why?

Art and culture in the Weimar Republic

During the 1920s, Germany replaced France as the cultural centre of Europe. German culture sparkled with creativity as artists experimented in photography, art, literature, cinema and architecture.

What were the cultural achievements of the Weimar period?

The term used to describe this remarkable cultural upheaval is 'Modernism'. Essentially, European artists and writers tried to break away from the artistic conventions of the 19th century to create new ways of seeing and interpreting the world. Not everything changed radically, however. Some trends continued from the years before 1914, such as the artistic movement known as Expressionism. Weimar culture was unique because, in a very short period, Germans experienced a multitude of avant-garde (experimental) movements and the rapid development of a 'mass culture' in the form of radio, cinema and the press.

Yet this rush to become 'modern' attracted bitter criticism from those, like the Nazis, who opposed the Republic. They condemned Modernism as being out of touch with the experience of ordinary Germans. For example, they disliked the new freedom in dress and social customs which women were now enjoying and blamed these on Jewish and Communist influences from the Soviet Union. In many ways it seemed that political and cultural developments were completely separate from and irrelevant to each other during the Weimar years. The liveliness and creativity of the cultural scene did little to win respect for the Republic as a political system or to stabilise it as a democracy.

American influences: music, cabaret and dance

In the 1920s, Germany opened up to foreign influences which had been kept out during the war years. American popular culture was welcomed; it was more 'democratic', more modern, and it celebrated living in the present rather than looking back to the past. Charlie Chaplin, black American cabaret groups, movies, jazz and boxing: all these were now part of the German cultural scene. The American dance, the Charleston, was the most popular dance in Germany in 1926. 'The Chocolate Kiddies' dance troupe performed in May 1925 and Josephine Baker, dancing nude to jazz music, was a smash hit with Berliners.

SOURCE A

Josephine Baker in the 1920s. Her cabaret performances were very popular in Germany.

SOURCE B

This poster appeared all over Berlin in 1921 to warn people about sexually transmitted diseases. It reads 'Berlin, stop and think! You are dancing with death!'

Literature

Some authors broke away from writing about traditional subjects. New novels dealt with topical themes such as the misery of urban life and, in the late Weimar period, the desperation felt by the unemployed. Novels were written on sexual themes and many contained bitter social comment. An example of the latter is the famous novel about the war written in 1929 and turned into a film the following year. *All Quiet on the Western Front* was written by Erich Maria Remarque and it contained a strong anti-war message. It was translated into 25 languages and it sold 3.5 million copies.

Architecture and design

In 1919, Walter Gropius founded the Bauhaus, a new school of architecture and design. It became famous for trying to break down the barriers between art and science. New and startling buildings were created and experimental designs were produced for furniture, lamps and pottery using different materials.

SOURCE C

The Einstein Tower near Potsdam. It was built in 1921 and was designed by one of the new architects, Erich Mendelsohn.

Cinema and photography

It is true that cinema had started to develop before the war, but it was during the 1920s that film-making and cinema-going really took off in Germany. Two million people went to the cinema every day; there were 2,300 film theatres in 1918 but 5,000 in 1930 (this was more than in any other European country); Germany produced more films than all the rest of Europe put together. Germany became famous for Expressionist fantasy films like Robert Wiene's *The Cabinet of Dr Caligari* (1920) and Fritz Lang's *Metropolis* (1926). American films were also shown and Charlie Chaplin was a particular favourite. Hollywood strengthened its commercial position when 'talkies' were introduced in 1928–29, but the German film industry responded and, in 1932, produced 127 sound films.

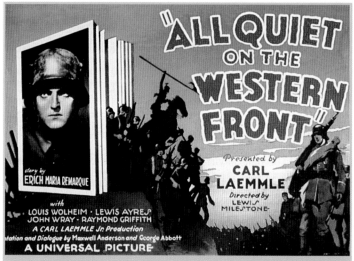

A poster for Hollywood's film version of Erich Maria Remarque's famous anti-war novel.

SOURCE D

This still is from The Cabinet of Dr Caligari, *directed by Robert Wiene in 1920. It shows Caligari's creature, Cesare, fleeing over nightmarish roof-tops with his victim in his arms.*

Radio

In 1923, the government gave permission for radio transmitters to be erected and for the manufacture of radio sets. This was a decisive turning point in public broadcasting. In 1924, nine radio companies covered the entire country. In April 1924 the number of listeners barely passed 10,000, but by April 1927 the total was 1.6 million and by April 1931 it had topped 3.7 million. In addition to music, listeners could hear radio plays and authors' readings.

SOURCE E

Changes in attitudes and life-style

The 1920s saw significant developments in the mass media – radio, press and cinema. The consequences of this new technology affected the lives and the outlook of broad sections of the population. Old taboos were cast off: sexual matters were more openly discussed; new horizons opened for people through sport, hiking and the development of clubs.

German culture at this time was deeply divided. Modernism was not the only feature of the cultural scene. The new forms of art were not universally accepted and traditional forms were still influential. Nevertheless, the label often attached to Weimar culture is that of the 'golden twenties' and it is easy to see why.

>> Activities

Use all the Sources and your knowledge of the period.

1 Which of these cultural achievements would Hitler and the Nazis not have approved of? Why?

2 Choose one of the forms of culture that interests you and carry out some research. Find out what was typical in that form in the years before 1914. Were the 1920s a turning point in its development or merely a continuation of what had gone before?

The Pillars of Society, 1926, by George Grosz criticises the leaders of Germany. This aggressive, modern style of painting was condemned by the Nazis. Compare it to the sentimental realism of the painting on page 54.

Was the Weimar Republic doomed from the start?

It might seem strange to undertake a review of the Weimar Republic at this point (1930) rather than at the moment when Hitler assumed power in January 1933. But many historians see 1930 and not 1933 as the year when the Weimar Republic ceased to exist. Their argument is that from 1930, President Hindenburg used the emergency powers available to him under Article 48 of the constitution to rule Germany by decree. From that moment on the Reichstag became irrelevant and German democracy was dead.

This review of the Weimar Republic takes the form of a historical debate which still rages today.

Some historians argue that the Weimar Republic was doomed from the start.

> The Weimar constitution contained two fatal flaws. Firstly, the voting system of proportional representation produced weak coalition governments which were unable to provide Germany with strong central government. Secondly, Article 48 gave President Hindenburg the power to destroy democracy.

> Democracy is not just a piece of paper laying out rules and rights. It must have deep roots if it is to survive crises. The Weimar Republic was born out of defeat and revolution and never had the support of most Germans.

> Although the 1918 revolution had swept the Kaiser away, much stayed the same. Many Germans in the army, the civil service, the police, the judiciary and the universities and schools did not like what the revolution had done and opposed democracy and the Republic.

> Weimar politicians were burdened with problems which hampered their efforts to give the Republic a good name. Many Germans blamed them, rightly or wrongly, for 'stabbing the army in the back' by signing the Armistice in November 1918; for the punishing Treaty of Versailles (1919) and the ongoing reparations; for the terrifying inflation of 1922–23; and for Germany's dependence on loans from the United States through the Dawes Plan (1924) and the Young Plan (1929).

Some historians argue that the Weimar Republic might have survived.

> The 1918 constitution was the best guarantee of individual liberties in Europe. Proportional representation is a voting system used in many countries today without problems; the same can be said of coalition governments. Furthermore, Article 48 was used successfully by President Ebert in dealing with the crises which arose in 1922–23.

> Democracy was nothing new in Germany in 1918. Under the old constitution, all males over 25 were allowed to vote for representatives in the parliament. The Social Democratic Party was established in 1875 and the Centre Party in 1870.

> The Weimar system and those politicians who had supported it had weathered all the crises between 1918 and 1923 and survived the taunts over their part in the Armistice and the Treaty of Versailles. If great German statesmen like Stresemann had still been alive, they could have rescued the Republic between 1930 and 1933.

> What destroyed the Weimar Republic was the crisis between 1930 and 1933. If the Depression had not hit Germany so severely and if the constitution had not been undermined, then the democracy established in 1918 could still be alive today.

The Depression, Nazi Germany and war

Germany, 1929–34: from democracy to dictatorship

These five years saw the death of the Weimar Republic and the establishment of Hitler's dictatorship, which was to last until his suicide in 1945.

Hitler was a political genius but he could not have been appointed Chancellor in January 1933 nor have established Nazi rule without help. In the difficult economic and social circumstances of the Great Depression, many longed for a return to strong authoritarian government similar to that provided by the Kaisers. Many people in Germany's political elite were looking around for someone to head this sort of government. Hitler was only one of several candidates, but the enormous success of the Nazi Party in elections during this period helped him to maintain a high political profile.

After several other Chancellors had been given a chance, President Hindenburg was persuaded to appoint Hitler. It was thought that he could be controlled; after all, his government contained only three Nazi ministers out of twelve. This was a serious miscalculation. Hitler took power with amazing speed. Within six months all organised forms of political opposition were destroyed. In the next six months he smashed what remained of the regional power of the Länder governments and in a further six months he had crushed opposition from within his own movement.

THE GREAT DEPRESSION 1929–33

By 1928, the economies of the world had become thoroughly integrated. The largest economy, that of the United States, was crucial in ensuring prosperity and jobs in Europe and other parts of the world. Germany, in particular, relied heavily on the United States after the Dawes Plan (1924). Huge loans helped restore the crisis-torn German economy and pay off reparations. While these loans lasted, most Germans had jobs and goods could be sold abroad. However, by 1928, the United States economy was starting to falter: the market for consumer goods had become saturated and factories were turning out products for which there was no demand. The Wall Street Crash in October 1929 worsened the situation; stocks and shares lost billions of dollars in value. Banks went bust as people drew out their money; companies and businesses who had lent money during the roaring 20s called in their loans. The loans to Germany had been short term and were called in quickly. Confidence evaporated overnight as factories shut down and businesses collapsed. It has been said that 'if America sneezes Europe catches a cold'. Germany's 'cold' was the worst in Europe. The Great Depression, which started in the United States, resulted in 6 million unemployed in Germany by 1933.

German children scavenge for food during the economic crisis of 1930.

Nazi Germany, 1934–39

Once in power, Hitler wanted all Germans to be one united national community and to cast aside the class, religious, political and regional differences which had characterised Weimar Germany. All aspects of life were co-ordinated to create this community around Nazi ideas and beliefs. Goebbels used propaganda to indoctrinate Germans; girls, boys, men and women all had their allotted place in the Nazi scheme of things. Of course, not every German was brainwashed. Many resisted in different ways. However, the changes Hitler made were popular: he got rid of the discredited parliamentary system; he provided strong rule; he gave Germans back their pride; and he reduced unemployment. It seemed he was their 'saviour'.

Hitler's second purpose was to deal with those who did not belong — in his eyes — to the national community of Germans. Many groups were persecuted throughout the 1930s. The Nazi view of race raised up the Aryan man and woman and damned everyone else.

Hitler's third purpose was to plan for war. He viewed war in global terms as a war between races (Aryan versus Slav) and considered war with the Soviet Union to be the inevitable final confrontation. The Slav race had been 'polluted' by the Jews, which is why the Soviet Union had 'fallen' to communism. Hitler saw communism as a 'Jewish disease'. In his mind there was bound to be a confrontation with the Soviet Union at some point, so Germany must be prepared for the conflict. Rearmament started; the armed forces grew in number and strength. The economy was stretched between two conflicting demands: preparing for war and satisfying the material needs of the German people.

Germany at war, 1939–45

Hitler's three aims were never explained in detail to the German people themselves. When war came, many feared the worst. After all, so much had been achieved peacefully. However, after early wartime successes in 1939–40, when much of Europe was in Nazi hands, Germans grew less fearful.

When the USA and the USSR joined the war in 1941 the tide turned against Hitler. Shortages hit many German households; accounts from the front undermined the propaganda that said all was well. Hitler was rarely seen in public after 1943 and his regime became unpopular. Attempts were made to assassinate him and to stop the war, but to no avail. With Soviet tanks crashing through the suburbs of Berlin in the spring of 1945, Hitler took his own life and Germany surrendered soon after. Hitler had said the Third Reich (the official Nazi name for their regime in Germany) would last a thousand years. In fact, it lasted only twelve, from 1933 to 1945.

A poster celebrating Hitler's vision of Germany: 'One People, One Reich, One Leader'.

Discussion points

> Why do you think Hitler only told the German people about his first two aims, but not the third?

> In what way was Hitler's rule different from that of the Weimar system?

Hitler comes to power

Since the Munich putsch in 1923 when Hitler failed to seize power by force, he had patiently bided his time. He reorganised the Nazi Party and followed the legal, democratic route to power. In 1933 his ten years of waiting came to an end: on 30 January he was appointed Chancellor. (This position is roughly equivalent to that of Prime Minister in Britain.)

Why did Hitler become Chancellor in 1933?

On one level, the answer to this question is easy: Hitler became Chancellor because President Hindenburg appointed him. But why is this not a satisfactory explanation? Firstly, it says nothing about why Hindenburg chose Hitler in preference to anyone else; secondly, it says nothing about Hindenburg's intentions and motives; thirdly, it says nothing about the beliefs and attitudes which shaped Hindenburg's intentions; and fourthly, it says nothing about why this event took place *when* it did. As you can see, 'why' questions in history can be complex.

In this investigation you will be looking at five questions. The answers, when put together, should give you a fairly complete explanation of Hitler's appointment, but first of all you need to have a clear picture of what happened in the fateful years, 1930–33.

President Hindenburg with Adolf Hitler in an open-top car during May Day celebrations in 1933.

GERMANY, 1930–33

In 1930 three important developments took place.

> Parliamentary government broke down and President Hindenburg ruled by decree, appointing and dismissing Chancellors as he wished.

> The Nazi Party became popular with the voters and was very successful in elections.

> Elite groups (army officers, owners of big business, the civil service and the big landowners) considered that their interests would best be served by a strong, authoritarian government rather than unstable coalition governments. In 1930, with the Depression deepening and the President acting alone, they were able to influence political decisions in ways which had not been possible before 1930.

A succession of Chancellors

President Hindenburg appointed Heinrich Brüning as Chancellor in 1930. Brüning did not need parliamentary support for his legislation, he simply needed Hindenburg to sign it. However, this system of rule by 'presidential cabinets' was always fragile. It depended upon the goodwill of Hindenburg and his advisers. Brüning's measures to try and deal with the effects of the Depression were unpopular and he resigned on 30 May 1932. The new Chancellor was Franz von Papen, a member of the Centre Party. Once again, unpopular laws were passed to cut back on welfare payments and von Papen too resigned.

A deal with Hitler

On 2 December 1932, von Schleicher became Chancellor. He tried to create some support for his government, but upset many groups by his discussions with trade union leaders. At this point, von Papen did a deal with Hitler: the Nazi leader would offer strong government with popular support (the many Nazi voters) and, in return, von Papen and his colleagues would form a majority of non-Nazis in the cabinet. Hindenburg was persuaded that in these circumstances Hitler could be controlled. Adolf Hitler was appointed Chancellor on 30 January 1933.

Question 1: What were Hitler's intentions?

From the time of the failed Munich putsch in 1923, Hitler's intention was to take power by any democratic method he could use. He wanted the position of Chancellor above all because only from that high office could he make decisions affecting the whole of Germany and have them enforced by authorities like the police, the army and his own SA.

Question 2: What were Hindenburg's intentions in appointing Hitler?

The evidence reveals that Hindenburg was hesitant about appointing Hitler as Chancellor. He had refused to appoint Hitler in August 1932 and again in November 1932, but he changed his mind only a few weeks later. In January 1933, Hindenburg was put under so much pressure that he agreed to appoint Hitler as long as his government contained a minority of Nazis. In this way Hitler could be tamed; or so he and von Papen thought.

Question 3: How did Hindenburg's beliefs and ideas shape his intentions and actions?

During the 1914–18 war Paul von Hindenburg had been joint head of the Supreme Command. In 1925 he was elected Reich President. He and some army friends deliberately set out to exploit the weaknesses in the procedure for forming parliamentary coalitions in order to build up the prestige and power of his own position as Reich President. He disliked democracy and considered that it led to weak government. His aim was to rewrite the Weimar constitution to make German government more authoritarian and less democratic. He blocked all attempts to pass laws to restrict the use of emergency powers under Article 48 of the constitution in order to keep a free hand for himself.

Question 4: What were the circumstances which made Hitler a suitable candidate for Chancellor?

A key factor here is the electoral success of the Nazi Party between 1930 and 1933. Indeed, it is easy to jump to the conclusion that this is why Hitler was appointed Chancellor. In fact, even if you look at the Nazi Party's best result in elections before Hitler took office, you will find that it only amounts to 37% of the vote. To put it another way, 63% of Germans voted for parties other than the Nazis even when they were at their most successful. Certainly, the Nazi Party did well but this only made Hitler one of several candidates for the post. Hindenburg did not have to appoint the leader of the most popular political party.

Nazi Party popularity stemmed from the issues they promoted in their propaganda. Speeches at impressive Nazi rallies, posters and leaflets played on themes such as nationalism and criticism of the Versailles treaty, and poured scorn on elements of left-wing politics: the KPD, SPD, the unions, labour law and welfare legislation.

SOURCE A

'We farmers are mucking out.' A Nationalist Socialist poster, 1932 election.

SOURCE B

This table shows the number of seats in the Reichstag won by the main parties in elections between 1928 and 1932.

	1928	1930	1932 July	1932 Nov.
Nazis	12	107	230	196
German Nationalist Party	73	41	37	52
German People's Party	45	30	7	11
Centre Party	62	68	75	70
German Democratic Party	25	20	4	2
Social Democratic Party	153	143	133	121
Communists	54	77	89	100
Other	67	91	33	32
Total	**491**	**577**	**608**	**584**

Unemployment

For other Germans, these issues were irrelevant in the context of their own desperate position as one of 6 million unemployed.

SOURCE C

Here are some grim calculations made by an employment exchange during 1931.

The average benefit paid to an unemployed man with a wife and a child was 51 marks a month. At least 32.50 marks went on rent, electricity, heating and other necessities. 18.50 marks remained to feed the family. Each person's daily rations consisted of six potatoes, five slices of bread, a handful of cabbage, a knob of margarine with a herring thrown in on three occasions during the month.

SOURCE D

This table shows the rising level of unemployment in Germany during the Depression.

Year	Number unemployed
1928	1,862,000
1929	2,850,000
1930	3,217,000
1931	4,886,000
1932	6,042,000

SOURCE E

An unemployed secretary advertises to passers-by: 'Hello, I'm looking for a job. I can do shorthand and typing. I can speak French and English and will accept any kind of household job...'

Question 5: How can the timing of Hitler's appointment be explained?

Between 1930 and 1933, the political and economic elites of German society were looking for an authoritarian replacement for the Weimar Republic. In this period, Hitler forged links with some of these leaders of business, industry and agriculture.

In November 1932 Hjalmar Schacht, a business leader, signed a petition to President Hindenburg requesting the appointment of Hitler as Chancellor. The President refused; he stuck by von Schleicher as his Chancellor. However, during the next few weeks, von Schleicher made some blunders which worried big business. Von Papen stepped in and liaised between big business, Schacht, the Nazi leadership and the group of advisers surrounding Hindenburg. The President finally agreed to appoint Hitler on the understanding that the government would be a conservative and not a Nazi one.

>> Activities

Use the Sources and the account of Germany, 1930–33.

1 Look again at questions **1** to **5**. Write an essay in two parts, answering these questions. What factors made it possible to appoint somebody like Hitler as Chancellor? What factors explain why Hitler was appointed on 30 January 1933?

2 In November 1932 the Social Democrats (SPD) and the Communists (KPD) together had more seats than the Nazis. Why didn't Hindenburg consider appointing someone from one of these parties to become Chancellor?

From democracy to dictatorship

It is astonishing how quickly Weimar democracy collapsed. Hitler took just 18 months, between February 1933 and August 1934, to establish his dictatorship. His first cabinet contained only three Nazis and, at the previous election in November 1932, the Nazi Party had managed to attract only 33% of the voters. So how and why was Hitler able to consolidate his position so quickly when he appeared to be so weak?

How did Hitler consolidate his power?

THE PATH TO DICTATORSHIP

1933

30 January	Hindenburg appoints Hitler as Chancellor.
27 February	The Reichstag building burns down.
28 February	Reichstag Fire Decree.
5 March	Reichstag election: Nazi Party gains 43.9% of the votes (288 seats), its coalition partners (the Nationalists) take 8%.
5–9 March	Nazis seize power in the Länder (German states).
20 March	Himmler establishes the first concentration camp at Dachau. *been there!*
23 March	Reichstag passes the Enabling Act.
2 May	Trade unions are dissolved.
22 June	SPD banned; other parties dissolve themselves in the weeks which follow.
14 July	Legislation prohibits political parties other than the Nazi Party.
12 November	New 'election' to the Reichstag; the Nazi Party gains 92.2% of the vote.

1934

30 June	'Night of the Long Knives' – Ernst Röhm and other SA leaders and members of the conservative opposition are arrested and shot without trial. *– eliminating rivals*
2 August	President Hindenburg dies. The offices of President and Chancellor are combined. Hitler is now called Führer (leader). The army swears an oath of allegiance to Hitler. *complete*

These extraordinary events can be explained by a number of different factors:

FACTOR 1

Politicians underestimated the strength of Hitler's position and misread his intentions.

Although there were only two other Nazis in Hitler's cabinet, one of them, Göring, held the key position of Minister of the Interior for Prussia. As such, he was in control of the police in Germany's biggest and most important state. Hitler's position was further strengthened because cabinet colleagues shared his desire to destroy left-wing influences and end parliamentary government. Finally, Hitler's SA was now some 2.5 million strong and eager to be unleashed upon political opponents. Far from being in a weak position in a cabinet dominated by non-Nazis, Hitler was in fact very powerful.

Hitler with SA Brownshirts at a rally in Dortmund, 1933.

Even when the Enabling Act was passed, transferring power to the cabinet and freeing government from dependence on the Reichstag, von Papen and his colleagues were not concerned. This is what they wanted: strong central government to replace weak, fumbling parliamentary rule. Unfortunately, what they did not see was that Hitler meant to carry the process further by using the same emergency powers to free himself from dependence not only on the Reichstag, but also on the President, the cabinet, his coalition partners and their parties.

FACTOR 2

Hitler ruthlessly exploited every opportunity to consolidate his power.

Hitler called elections for 5 March 1933 in the hope of bolstering the Nazi Party and his own position as Chancellor. In the weeks leading up to the election, action was taken to destroy the left-wing parties. Hitler was ruthless. On 4 February a decree banned newspapers and public meetings from criticising Hitler's government. In the middle of the month, Göring let loose 50,000 Stormtroopers in Prussia; an orgy of violence against Socialists and Communists took place.

On 27 February, one week before election day, the Reichstag building went up in flames. A young Dutch Communist called Marinus van der Lubbe was caught at the scene in possession of firelighters. Under interrogation, he claimed he had acted alone. Historians debate this version of events. Most accept van der Lubbe's confession that he acted alone; a few argue that the Nazis set him up to take the blame for the fire which they themselves started. The truth may never be known but what is certain is that the Nazis used the incident in a propaganda

Propaganda masters

Van der Lubbe on trial, 1933.

campaign to whip up fears of a Communist uprising. Göring used it to justify the violent actions of the SA against political opponents, and concentration camps sprang up all over Germany.

The day after the fire, the Reichstag Fire Decree was introduced suspending all personal rights and freedoms. Political prisoners could now be held for unlimited periods without having to appear in court. By April, 25,000 were in custody in Prussia alone. The Enabling Act followed on 23 March. This allowed the government to pass laws without consulting the Reichstag and without the authority of President Hindenburg. Most Germans took the threat of a Communist uprising very seriously and accepted Hitler's drastic measures.

FACTOR 3

The Nazis made widespread use of violence to crush political opposition.

The Stormtroopers had long awaited their chance to settle old scores from previous street-battles with political enemies. Revenge and hatred fed their lust for violence against so-called German 'traitors' like Communists, Socialists, Jews, Catholic priests and journalists. Police often stood by and watched, quietly applauding the SA's brutality.

SOURCE A

This photograph was taken in 1933 after Hitler had become Chancellor. It shows the arrest of Communists in Berlin.

FACTOR 4

Hitler dealt swiftly and efficiently with the threat to his own position from within the Nazi Party.

Hitler knew it would be dangerous to upset army leaders. They could become a focus for opposition. When they voiced their concerns about the SA as a threat to the army, Hitler showed himself ready to act ruthlessly. The 'bully boys' had outlived their usefulness to Hitler. Now he was in power their hooligan behaviour was unnecessary in creating an ordered Nazi state. Hitler struck swiftly. On 30 June 1934, SA leaders were arrested by the Gestapo and immediately shot. Ernst Röhm, the SA leader, was among the 85 victims. Hitler justified this 'Night of the Long Knives' on the grounds that Röhm was plotting to overthrow the government. Hindenburg said that Hitler had 'saved the nation'. The episode not only removed opposition within the Nazi movement, it also showed would-be opponents that the regime was absolutely ruthless in its use of force whenever it was threatened.

A few weeks later, following Hindenburg's death in August 1934, all soldiers swore an oath of loyalty to Hitler personally.

FACTOR 5

The opposition was so weak and divided that it could do nothing to stop Hitler.

Those organisations which could have opposed Hitler were stunned by the speed and surprise of the attacks upon them. The trade union movement, for example, was eliminated in March and April of 1933 in piecemeal fashion. First one town and then another saw their union buildings raided and closed down. Breslau, Dresden, Frankfurt and Hanover were picked off one at a time. No one could say when or where the next blow might be struck; no one knew when or how to make a stand.

In the city of Breslau the two opposition political parties – the KPD and the SPD – failed to join forces against the Nazis, a sad reflection of the bitterness between the two which had begun during the revolution in 1918.

SOURCE B

Ernst Röhm, the leader of the SA.

SOURCE C

This is part of a description of what happened in the city of Breslau on 31 January 1933. It is taken from a book called Life in the Third Reich *(1987), edited by the historian, Richard Bessel.*

The Communists reacted to the news of Hitler's appointment by arranging for a protest demonstration in the city centre at which a general strike was to be announced. At the appointed time when Communist supporters began to assemble, about 500 Stormtroopers decided to march through the square. The police kept about 500–600 Communist supporters out of the square while the SA paraded around; when the planned demonstration did start, the police quickly intervened to stop it. Police truncheons appeared and Communists scattered, some running up nearby streets and smashing the windows of shops selling Nazi uniforms. The SPD in Breslau had adopted a 'wait and see' attitude; they saw the results of the Communist demonstrations as justifying their own decision to do nothing.

FACTOR 6

The political elites co-operated with the Nazi regime.

Most members of the civil service felt at home with the nationalist, authoritarian style of Hitler's rule. They were prominent amongst those seeking to protect their positions and pensions by joining the Nazi Party. Similarly, most German judges and lawyers welcomed Hitler's strong, forceful government. The Reich Justice Minister, Franz Gürtner, was a conservative and not a Nazi, yet he was happy to back the illegal activities of the Nazis. He argued that they were necessary in very unusual circumstances.

You have already read about how other elites conspired to wreck Weimar democracy and replace it with a strong ruler. Now they had one: Adolf Hitler was a dictator within 18 months of being appointed Chancellor.

SOURCE D

Nazi Stormtroopers occupy trade union offices in Munich, 1933.

>> Activities

Study all the Sources and use your background knowledge.

1 Draw a table like this and fill it in for the period 1933–34, when Hitler consolidated his power.

Individual/ Group	Actions/ Decisions	Intentions/ Motives	Attitudes/ Beliefs
Hitler			
von Papen			
van der Lubbe			
Army			
Communists			
Social Democrats			
Trade unionists			
Civil servants			
Judges			

Which of the groups/individuals followed a course of action which had unintended consequences? Which of these was the most serious in allowing Hitler to consolidate his power?

Which of the groups/individuals could have prevented Hitler from consolidating his power? When and how could they have done so?

2 Using the information from the completed table and your answers to the other tasks, write an essay to explain why Hitler was able to consolidate his power so quickly. Structure it by referring to all the groups in the table and dividing them into those who supported Hitler and those who opposed him.

1930–34: Hitler's rise to power

PLANNING AND PREPARATION DURING THE 1920s

> Hitler tried and failed to take power by force so had to bide his time and use democratic methods.

> After he came out of prison, Hitler re-organised the Nazi Party and consolidated his leadership of it.

> He dropped the part of the Nazi Party programme which mentioned taking control of private property; from then on, it was only Jewish property which was in danger.

> He changed the Nazi Party from a small organisation to one which by 1928 was ready to be a mass party.

> Membership of the SA grew steadily.

WHY WEREN'T THE NAZIS POPULAR DURING THE 1920s?

> The government survived the crises of 1923 and, under statesmen like Stresemann, Germany seemed to be more stable.

> The huge loans given to Germany under the Dawes Plan in 1924 enabled the economy to recover from the hyper-inflation of 1922–23.

> Voters saw nothing in the Nazi programme which attracted them.

> Most Germans had the necessities of life (food, housing, etc.).

WHY DID THE NAZIS GAIN POPULARITY BETWEEN 1930 AND 1933?

> The Great Depression created 6 million unemployed.

> Nazi propaganda from Goebbels worked effectively.

> Hitler had not been part of any Weimar government and could ask voters to give him a chance, as they had given the other parties.

> The Nazi Party was now receiving support from across the classes.

> The party received some financial support from industry.

However, Hitler and the Nazis were never supported by a majority of the German voters between 1930 and 1933. More people voted against the Nazis than in favour of them.

HOW WAS HITLER ABLE TO TAKE POWER IN 1933?

> Backstairs intrigue involving von Papen and Hindenburg.

> Political and economic elites wanted democracy to be shelved in favour of strong authoritarian government.

> Since 1930, democracy had already been killed off by President Hindenburg's use of emergency powers under Article 48 of the constitution, which allowed him to pass decrees without reference to the Reichstag.

HOW WAS HITLER ABLE TO CONSOLIDATE POWER?

> Opposition was weak, split and badly organised.

> The SA ruled the streets with violence and terror.

> Many Germans actually approved of Hitler's strong leadership even if some minorities suffered.

> Hitler completely outmanoeuvred those in his non-Nazi cabinet who thought he could be controlled. He created a dictatorship under their noses.

> Hitler was careful not to upset the army, who could oppose him, but he was ruthless in eliminating the threat in his own ranks from Röhm and the Stormtroopers.

Prominent Nazis

Joseph Goebbels (1897–1945)

Born in 1897, Goebbels contracted polio as a child which left him with a club-foot. This deformity disqualified him from serving in the First World War. He studied history and literature at university and in 1922 he joined the Nazi Party.

In the Third Reich, Goebbels was Reich Minister of Propaganda between 1933 and 1945. He had control of all branches of the media and the arts. His aim was to mobilise Germans behind Hitler and his government. Goebbels was a brilliant speaker and his radio broadcasts reached into every German home. Propaganda became increasingly important during the war years when the Nazi regime had to prepare Germans to make huge sacrifices. Although Germany was losing the war, Goebbels remained loyal to Hitler right to the end. He died with his wife and family in Hitler's bunker in Berlin on 1 May 1945.

Hermann Göring (1893–1946)

Göring was born in Bavaria in 1893 and attended the military cadets' college at Karlsruhe. He joined the army in 1914 as an infantry lieutenant before being transferred to the airforce as a combat pilot. Göring was an ace pilot and won the Iron Cross (First Class) for exceptional bravery. After the war, Göring settled in Munich and met Hitler in 1922. He was appointed head of the SA (Stormtroopers) and led them from December 1922 until the Munich putsch. Göring was seriously wounded in the putsch but escaped abroad. In 1927 he rejoined the Nazi Party and was elected to the Reichstag in 1928. In 1932 he became first the Speaker and then the President of the Reichstag. In 1933 he was Prussian Minister of the Interior and played a key role in the seizure of power and the arrests of Communists and Socialists. He acted ruthlessly against Ernst Röhm and the SA in June 1934 in the Night of the Long Knives. In 1935 he was put in charge of the Air Force (the Luftwaffe) and in

1936 Hitler made him responsible for the Four Year Plan which laid down preparations for war. The failure of the Luftwaffe, the Allied bombing raids on Germany and Göring's own addiction to drugs resulted in his downfall. By 1945 he had lost all influence. At the Nuremberg Trials in 1945 he was condemned to death by hanging. He took poison in 1946 while awaiting execution.

Heinrich Himmler (1900–45)

Heinrich Himmler was an agricultural graduate and a poultry farmer. He had an obsession with detail and accuracy and during the Holocaust this revealed itself in his meticulous collection of statistics of murdered Jews. Early on in his political career he was involved in the Munich putsch of 1923. His loyalty to Hitler was rewarded: in 1929 he became head of Hitler's personal bodyguard, the SS. The SS became a racial elite with responsibility for killing the Jews. Himmler did more than any other single Nazi to carry out the 'Final Solution' by setting up the death camps in which millions of people were exterminated. He was arrested by the British on 23 May 1945 and took his own life.

Reinhard Heydrich (1904–42)

Reinhard Heydrich was Himmler's subordinate. He had the looks of an Aryan German and tried to keep secret the fact that he had Jewish ancestors. Heydrich joined the Nazi Party and, at the age of 27, became chief of the security services. Using spies, this organisation collected personal information on all of the leading Nazis and their opponents. When Hitler came to power, Heydrich was ready to cast his network of spies all over the country and his responsibilities included running the Gestapo under Himmler's overall command. In 1941 he was one of the foremost Nazis involved in organising the 'Final Solution'. He was assassinated in Prague by Czech freedom fighters in May 1942.

Coercion and consent

The previous investigation showed how some of the Nazis' political opponents were quickly dealt with: locked up in concentration camps, tortured, murdered, or exiled. It would be wrong, however, to exaggerate the extent of opposition to Hitler. Certainly, there was repression and coercion, but there was also consent for what Hitler was doing from many of the 66 million Germans. Who agreed with what Hitler was doing? Who opposed him? How were they treated?

How effectively did the Nazis deal with their political opponents?

Selective repression

Coercion and consent were the twin props of Hitler's power. Powerful groups such as industrialists, landowners and bankers were left alone. Jews were terrorised as were gypsies, homosexuals and beggars. Police harassment was concentrated in working-class rather than middle-class areas of big cities. There was no assault on farmers in the countryside. Nazi repression was aimed at the powerless and unpopular sections of society.

Communists, Socialists and trade unionists were unpopular with the German upper- and middle-classes, who were pleased to see Hitler break up the organisations and arrest their leaders. Levels of repression were not constant. After 1934–35, when organised opposition was violently crushed, there was a lull until 1937–39, when the persecution of the Jews and other 'undesirables' grew more savage. At this point, Hitler was busy preparing for war.

The Church and political opposition

In the early 1930s, the Catholic and Protestant Churches had co-operated with the Nazi state. Hitler had signed an agreement, known as a Concordat, with the Catholic Church in July 1933. This promised full religious freedom to Catholics in return for loyalty to the Nazi state. But the Nazis broke the agreement and responded to Catholic protests about Nazi interference in the life of the Church and violations of human rights by sending hundreds of clergy to concentration camps. The Nazi regime also persecuted Protestants who resisted state interference in Church matters. In 1937, 800 pastors were arrested and many were sent to concentration camps.

The price of resistance

Resistance from groups hostile to the Nazi regime never ceased. Thousands of people from all walks of life suffered persecution, imprisonment, and sometimes death, for defying the Nazis. Between 1933 and 1939, courts sentenced 225,000 people to a total of 600,000 years' imprisonment for political offences. Between 1933 and 1945, 3 million Germans were held at one time or another in prison or camps on political grounds or for active resistance.

SOURCE A

Political prisoners in Dachau concentration camp.

SOURCE B

From An Honourable Defeat, *a history book written in 1994 by Anton Gill.*

Otto Bauer, a 56-year-old businessman, said on a train in June 1942 that Germans only had two alternatives: to kill Hitler or be killed by him. He was overheard by a married couple who reported him. He was beheaded on 16 September 1943 for causing discontent and unrest.

Erich Deibel: on 29 April 1940 he drew the symbol of the SPD – three arrows – on the wall of the lavatory in his factory, adding the words: 'Hail Freedom!' On 22 July the following year he chalked up: 'Workers! Help Russia! Strike! Up with the Communist Party!' and drew the red star and the hammer and sickle. He also listened to broadcasts from the BBC. Accused of sabotage and treason, he was executed on 15 August 1942.

Nazi law enforcement

The SS (Schutz Staffel) was established in 1925 as a personal bodyguard for Hitler. Its duties were very similar to the SA during the 1920s. But in 1929, Heinrich Himmler took it over and built up numbers from 200 to 50,000. They acquired a black uniform to distinguish them from the SA. Initially they were subordinate to the SA, but this all changed after the Night of the Long Knives. As a reward for their services in purging the SA, Hitler made the SS an independent organisation inside the Nazi Party. In 1936, Hitler amalgamated all the separate police forces into one organisation and placed it under Himmler's control. This included an organisation called the Gestapo (Geheime Staatspolizei or secret police).

The Gestapo had been set up in 1933 by Göring. Its purpose was to discover the enemies of the Nazi state using whatever means they thought necessary; in other words they could break the law. Arrests late at night, interrogation, torture, internment and sometimes death: these were the hallmarks of the Gestapo operations. They instilled fear in those thinking of resistance. They were helped in their task by the Malicious Practices Act of 21 March 1933, which banned criticism of Hitler and the Nazi state. Denouncers and snoopers informed on their fellow citizens. Without the support of these 'loyal Germans' the capacity of the Gestapo to keep people under control would have been very much reduced.

SOURCE D

These statistics for three German cities in 1937 show the relatively low level of policing by the Nazis:

City	Population	Number of Gestapo officers
Düsseldorf	500,000	126
Essen	650,000	43
Würzburg	840,000	22

SOURCE E

Here are some statistics about the German population in 1933.

Total population: 66 million
Percentage of Jews: 1%
Percentage living in cities over 100,000: 30%
Percentage living in small rural communities of less than 2,000: 32%

SOURCE C

A recruiting poster for the Waffen SS, the military branch of the SS.

>> **Activities**

Use all the Sources and your background knowledge.

1 What do the Sources suggest were the reasons why many Germans did not resist Hitler?

2 Using the statistical evidence from these Sources do you think Hitler relied more on coercion than consent or vice versa?

Propaganda

Terror and propaganda: these were the two weapons the Nazis used to control the German people. You studied Nazi terror in the previous investigation; propaganda is the focus of this one.

How did the Nazis use culture and the mass media to control the people?

Propaganda is not just telling lies to change ideas and attitudes; it is more complicated than that. Very often propaganda reinforces existing beliefs by giving them a sharper focus. Propaganda can be the outright lie, the half truth, or the truth taken out of its context, or indeed a mixture of all three. During the Nazi period both culture and the mass media were controlled to help build a unified national community based on Nazi values. How was this done? What were the propaganda messages?

The purposes of Nazi propaganda

For Hitler and Goebbels, propaganda had one prime function: to reshape people's beliefs, values and ideas along Nazi lines. Germans were told time and time again about 'racial purity'; the need to create 'national solidarity'; and the importance of trusting Hitler's leadership.

SOURCE A

This diagram shows the different purposes of Nazi propaganda and how they are linked together.

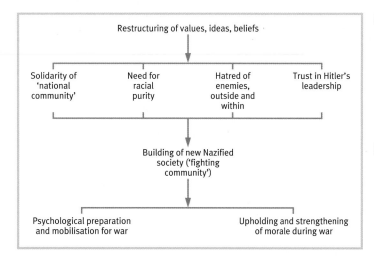

Controlling culture

Goebbels established the Reich Chamber of Culture and his Ministry for Propaganda in 1933. The Reich Chamber had sections dealing with newspapers, film, art, radio, literature, theatre and music. Germans wanting to work in any of these areas had to be members of the Chamber. Membership depended on supporting the Nazis: if you did not support the Nazis, your work could not be performed or published. Many creative people went abroad to work.

Censorship

Nazi versions of events were given to the public to read. Goebbels censored what newspapers could print and had shut down 1,600 newspapers by the end of 1934. Germany's 10,000 magazines and journals suffered too; half had disappeared by 1938.

Literature

The Nazis organised the burning of books whose authors were Jewish, unsympathetic to Nazi ideals, or both. In May 1933 Berlin students ceremonially set fire to a huge pile of 20,000 books which had been looted from libraries. In the pile were books by some of Germany's most famous authors. The works of over 2,500 writers were officially banned.

Radio

In 1932 there were 4.5 million radios in Germany. Ten years later there were over 16 million. A radio cost an average week's wages. Hitler made 50 broadcasts in his first year in office. Sets were placed in factories and cafés, and loudspeakers were installed in streets.

Music

The work of Jewish composers was banned and so was jazz because it was written by black Americans. Viennese music by Strauss was played most frequently along with the heroic German operas of Wagner.

SOURCE B

'Yes! Leader we will follow you!' A propaganda poster intended to encourage mass support for Hitler.

SOURCE C

This cartoon was published in the Westfälische Landeszeitung, a German newspaper, in January 1939. It shows two maps of Germany. The top one represents Weimar Germany, the bottom one, Nazi Germany.

Cinema

Cinema attendances topped 250 million in 1933. This figure quadrupled in the next ten years. The Nazi film industry produced about 100 films a year. About half were comedies and love stories and a quarter were musicals or thrillers. The remainder had historical, military or political themes or were films for the young. One of the best known was *Hitlerjunge Quex* (1933), which tells the story of a boy who broke away from a Communist family to join the Hitler Youth only to be murdered by the Communists.

>> Activities

1 Study Sources B and C. What messages are these images trying to communicate? (Use Source A to help you.)

2 Do Sources B and C contain **a** outright lies; **b** half truths; **c** truths taken out of context; or **d** a mixture of all three?

3 Given what you know about political opposition to the Nazis, how successful does Nazi propaganda appear to have been?

Nazi persecution

The Nazis began the persecution of minorities soon after they took power in 1933. Jews suffered the most and endured the greatest losses: over 6 million were systematically killed in what is known as the Holocaust. The Nazis planned to kill all the Jews they found so that they could create an 'Aryan' order in Europe. Other groups that suffered under the Nazis were gypsies, homosexuals, mentally and physically disabled people, Slavs, Jehovah's Witnesses, Socialists and Communists.

Why did the Nazis persecute different minority groups in Germany?

SOURCE A

A Nazi sculpture of the ideal Aryan.

Nazi ideas on race

Hitler believed not in the human race but in human races and the differences between them. The 'Aryan' race, in Hitler's mind, was superior to all other races in terms of physical strength, intelligence and cultural achievements. The ideal Aryan would be tall with blond hair and blue eyes. This was the ideal; it was obvious that not all Germans matched these features. Aryans were the most valuable race, and if they interbred with 'less valuable races' they were doomed to extinction. To prevent this from happening, the purity and health of the Aryan race had to be protected and improved. In practice, this would mean increasing the number of babies of 'Aryan stock' and reducing the number from 'inferior stock'. These ideas were not just Hitler's, nor were they new; plenty of ordinary Germans shared them.

The persecution of Jews

Anti-Semitism was commonplace in Europe during the 1920s. In 1922, Walter Rathenau, the Jewish German Foreign Minister, was murdered by racists. Between 1922 and 1933 there were 200 incidents in Nuremberg alone of Jewish

SOURCE B

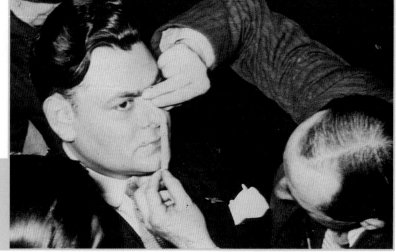

Government officials measure a man's nose to find out if he is an Aryan or not. Nazis believed that tests like these could be used to check a person's 'racial purity'.

graves being desecrated. *Der Stürmer*, the Nazi newspaper, was first published in 1923; its slogan was 'The Jews are our greatest misfortune'.

On coming to power, the Nazis at once set about excluding 'non-Aryans' (Jews) from public life. The Nazis defined 'non-Aryans' as persons with a Jewish parent or grandparent. Jews were banished from the civil service and from teaching in schools and universities, and barred from practising as doctors, dentists and judges. These measures were widely accepted by the majority of the German public. Jews were deprived of opportunities to work in the economy and to take part in German civic and cultural life. The main thrust of Nazi policy was to wage a legal war of attrition so as to make life so unbearable for Jews that they would leave Germany 'voluntarily'.

Many of Germany's 550,000 Jews did emigrate and more would have done so had other countries been more helpful. In July 1938, 33 governments were represented at the Evian Conference to discuss the refugee situation, but only a few agreed to accept more Jewish immigrants.

Once the war started in 1939, Nazi persecution of the Jews intensified. When the Nazis conquered Poland, Jews were herded into ghettos where they lived in the most appalling and dehumanising conditions. The Warsaw ghetto was the largest of all: half a million people were crammed into 1.3 square miles; the average room held seven people; and only one in every hundred flats had running water. Disease was rife.

SOURCE C

From April 1933 Nazi Stormtroopers organised and enforced a boycott of all Jewish-owned shops and businesses.

March 1933	Department of Racial Hygiene established.
April 1933	Nationwide boycott of Jewish shops; laws passed to dismiss non-Aryans from public service and the professions.
1935 Nuremberg Laws	Jews lose their rights as German citizens. It became illegal for Jews to marry, or to have any relations with, Aryans. Jews were encouraged to leave Germany.
1938 Kristallnacht	Mass destruction of synagogues and shops; about a thousand Jews were murdered and many arrested.
1938	Jewish businesses taken over by Nazis.
1942–45	The Holocaust.

In June 1941 the Germans invaded the Soviet Union. A month later an order was signed by Goering to make the necessary preparations for a 'Final Solution to the Jewish problem'. The *Einsatzgruppen* (killing squads) went into action in the newly conquered Soviet territories. Sometimes, with the help of local volunteers, they killed local Jews and buried them in mass graves.

It soon became clear that the methods used by the *Einsatzgruppen* were unable to cope with the large numbers of people whom the Nazis deemed to be 'sub-human', so a more efficient method was found. At the Chelmo camp a mobile gas van was used to kill up to 40 people in one operation. Carbon monoxide from the exhaust pipes was pumped into the back of sealed vans. Over 200,000 Polish Jews were killed in this way as well as tens of thousands of Soviet prisoners.

In 1942 at the Wannsee Conference, leading Nazis agreed on a plan for the 'Final Solution to the Jewish problem'. The persecution of the Jews in Nazi Germany had now reached its last and most terrifying stage. By 1942, the Nazis had invaded many of the countries to which Jews had fled from Germany in the 1930s. The 'Final Solution' decided upon in 1942 was simple: when Jews were found, they were rounded up and then transported to death camps in the occupied countries. This applied to every single Jew in Europe. Many perished in the gas chambers at Auschwitz, where Zyklon B was used to poison them. Corpses were disposed of in large ovens which burned day and night to cope with the huge numbers. Historians estimate that between 5 and 6 million Jews were murdered. Hitler's role was central to the slaughter.

The persecution of the mentally and physically disabled

For many years this group of people was thought of as inferior by some scientists, zoologists and doctors. Euthanasia and sterilisation were two suggested 'remedies'. Many would have echoed the thoughts of Ernst Haeckel in Source D.

SOURCE D

From The Riddle of Life *written by German zoologist, Ernst Haeckel (1834–1919), in 1904.*

What profit does humanity gain from the thousands of cripples who are born each year, from the deaf and dumb, from cretins, from those with incurable hereditary defects who are kept alive artificially and then raised to adulthood? What a lot of pain they suffer! What a lot of money it costs to look after them! All of this could be avoided with a dose of morphine.

During the 1920s, debates about sterilisation resurfaced because the 1914–18 war had killed so many young men – those considered to be the 'most valuable' human stock. In 1923, the Zwickau District Health Officer announced that surgeons in his district were already sterilising mentally disabled people, illegally. During the Depression, governments cut spending on welfare, which included the care of the disabled. In July 1932 the Prussian state government had drafted a Sterilisation Law. Even before 1933, disabled people were already thought of as dispensable by some in German society.

January 1934	Law for the Prevention of Hereditarily Diseased Children – this law allowed sterilisation of diseased children. Over 360,000 sterilisations had been carried out by 1945.
October 1939	Euthanasia Order – its aim was to kill German mental patients. Special hospitals were established where disabled children were murdered usually by poison or starvation. Later, children who had malformed ears or who wet the bed were included. The killing of disabled adults soon followed.

SOURCE E

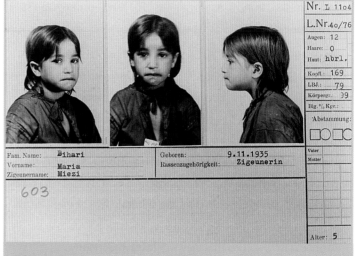

Photographs of a gypsy girl kept on a Nazi file.

The persecution of the Sinti and Roma (gypsies)

When the Nazis came to power they inherited Länder (state) laws which discriminated against the Sinti and Roma. The Bavarian authorities had kept a register of them from 1899, and from 1911 added fingerprints to it. In 1926 a new law enabled the police to send Sinti and Roma people to workhouses for two years if they did not have regular work. Under the Nazis, the Sinti and Roma were confined to designated sites after 1939. Those who tried to leave were sent to concentration camps where they were very badly treated.

1941 marked the change from persecution to extermination. 250,000 Sinti and Roma were shot in Russia, Poland and the Balkans. In December 1942 those living in Germany were sent to Auschwitz. Out of the 23,000 sent, 20,078 perished.

The persecution of homosexuals and black people

Homosexuals and black people were persecuted by the Nazis because they endangered the development of an 'Aryan order' in Europe. Homosexuals could not have children, and black people were close to Jews in the Nazi view of the 'human races'.

Laws against homosexuality had been in place since 1871, but during the Weimar period there were signs that persecution might end: a gay press flourished and in Berlin and Hamburg homosexuality was tolerated. Hitler brought these developments to an end. In February 1933 homosexual groups were banned. Large numbers of homosexuals were arrested towards the end of 1934 and in 1936 a law was passed to have all homosexuals sterilised.

In the 1920s many black soldiers came to an area of Germany called the Rhineland as part of the French army of occupation under the terms of the Treaty of Versailles. Many of the black soldiers from Senegal and Morocco formed relationships with local German women. The children born of these couples were called 'Rhineland bastards' by the Weimar press and then the Nazi regime. Instead of curbing the racist reactions of politicians and journalists, the Weimar authorities themselves collected information on the number, names and location of these children. In 1937 the Nazis used this information to track down and sterilise 385 children without them or their parents knowing what was going on.

Jesse Owens, a black American athlete, won four gold medals at the 1936 Berlin Olympic Games. His achievement undermined the Nazi belief in the superiority of Aryan athletes and Hitler refused to congratulate Owens.

>> Activities

1 What did the Nazis mean by 'Aryan race'? How can the Nazi vision of Germany's future help to explain their treatment of minorities?

2 Scientists (like Ernst Haeckel, Source D) and doctors suggested that some groups of people were more valuable than others.

   a How did these views help justify the actions of the persecutors?

   b Article 104 of the Weimar Constitution guaranteed equality before the law for all Germans, yet racism existed during the 1920s. Can you explain this contradiction?

3 Use the Sources and the timecharts to make a list of all the individuals and groups who appear to have treated Germans unequally. What does this tell you about the extent of racism in Germany?

4 '1933 was more a continuation of existing policy than a turning point in the way German authorities treated minorities.' To what extent do you agree with this?

Totalitarianism?

The term 'totalitarianism' was first coined in Italy in May 1923 as a term of abuse against Mussolini's Fascist government. In England in 1929 the term was used to describe both Fascist (Italy and later Germany) and Communist (Soviet Union) states.

Was Nazi Germany a totalitarian state?

After the purge of the SA in June 1934, there were three and a half years of political peace in Germany. This allowed the Nazis time to 're-model' German society according to their values and beliefs. In theory, all areas of German life had to be re-organised: no individual or group could avoid this process. German men and women were to be accountable for their thoughts and feelings as well as for their actions. The demands of the Nazi Party and the State were to be more important than the rights of the individual.

In practice, however, Nazi Germany turned out to be rather different:

> Until the outbreak of war, Germany was still open to visitors and foreign journalists – unlike the Soviet Union.

> The Nazis were sensitive to hostile comments from abroad: for example, foreign criticism of Nazi policy made Hitler stop those in the Party who wished to take extreme measures against the Churches.

> The ways in which the Nazis enforced their style of government changed dramatically after the outbreak of war. In 1939, for example, the number of prisoners in concentration camps was about 25,000 out of a total population of 66 million. A few years later, during the war, the number had increased to about 250,000.

> The Nazi government was not united. No one questioned Hitler's authority at the top, but there were fierce struggles for power in the ranks beneath him. Each government minister and Nazi Party official fought for their own interests and the favour of the Führer. This strengthened Hitler's own position but weakened the control of the Nazi government.

Carl Friedrich, a political thinker, described six features which totalitarian states possess:

> an official ideology (a fixed way of thinking)

> a single mass party

> police control based upon terror

> total control over the media

> total control over arms

> central control over the economy

>> Activity

Using Friedrich's six features of a totalitarian state and information you have obtained about Nazi Germany, make a list of those aspects of the Nazi state which were 'totalitarian' and make a second list of those aspects which were not. Was Nazi Germany a 'totalitarian' state or not?

There was no place for opposition in Nazi Germany. This 1934 cartoon by the British cartoonist David Low is a comment on the 'Night of the Long Knives' when the SA was eliminated.

Young people in Nazi Germany

In Hitler's eyes the young were particularly important. They had to be won over so that Hitler's policies could be implemented. To create a racial state, the Nazis had to indoctrinate children to believe in the superiority of the Aryan, the 'master race'. To fight a 'race war' against the Soviet Union, young men had to cherish the military ideals of discipline, sacrifice and obedience. Cementing together these two aims was the Führer: all young Germans were taught to see him as a father-figure who demanded and should receive unquestioning loyalty from his people.

How did young people react to the Nazi regime?

SOURCE A

Hitler with a small boy dressed up as the SA mascot.

SOURCE B

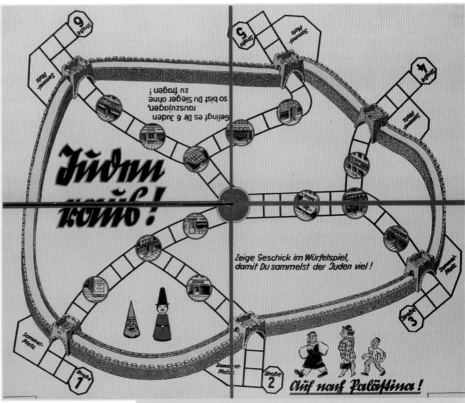

A children's board game called 'Get the Jews out'. The child who chased six Jews from their businesses and homes was the winner. The instructions read: 'Be skilful when you throw the dice and you'll gather Jews in a trice. If you succeed in throwing six Jews out, you're the winner without a doubt!' This game sold one million copies in 1938, the year that Nazi policy towards Jews encouraged emigration.

Education

At school young Germans were faced with a National Curriculum devised by the Nazis. The teaching of school subjects was changed to indoctrinate pupils. History was distorted to celebrate German victories during the Great War and to downplay the achievements of the Weimar Republic by teaching about the 'betrayal' of 1918, the humiliation of Versailles, and the inflation of 1923. All disasters were, of course, blamed on the Communists and the Jews. Biology lessons were devoted to studying the differences between races and maths problems contained facts and figures about looking after the disabled in ways which made them seem dispensable.

It would be wrong, however, to think that all young Germans were brainwashed and believed everything they were taught. Plenty did not. In practice, young people learned from lots of different influences both in and out of school. Some used Hitler Youth duties as an excuse to miss school and vice versa.

SOURCE C

This picture is from a children's book. It shows Jewish children being taken out of the school by their teacher. The 'Aryan' teacher stands watching in the background.

SOURCE D

This extract is taken from the memoirs of a German who was a student during the Nazi period.

No one in our class ever read *Mein Kampf*. I myself had only used the book for quotations. In general we didn't know much about Nazi ideas. Anti-Semitism wasn't mentioned much by teachers except through Richard Wagner's essay 'The Jews in Music'.

In spite of all the Nazis' best efforts through their National Curriculum, research seems to show that Nazi education had no universal effects on young Germans.

The Hitler Youth

This organisation had been running since 1925 and in the first few years after 1933 many young people joined voluntarily. It offered a variety of leisure pursuits. This was particularly welcomed in rural areas where the arrival of the Hitler Youth meant a first chance to join any kind of youth organisation. Boys and girls could now enjoy weekend trips, walking and sports. Indeed, the League of German Girls offered some the chance to break free from the female role model of child-care and devotion to family.

SOURCE F

This extract is from the memoirs of Marianne MacKinnon, a member of the League of German Girls.

I was not thinking of the Führer when I gave the Nazi salute, but of games, sports, hiking, singing, camping and other exciting activities. Many young people like me had a thirst for action and found it in the Hitler Youth. Almost everything took the form of competitions. Not only were there contests for the best performances in sport and at work, but each unit wanted to have the best-kept home, or the most interesting travel album.

SOURCE E

This table shows membership figures for the various sections of the Hitler Youth.

	HJ (boys aged 14–18)	DJ (boys aged 10–14)	BDM (girls aged 14–18)	JM (girls aged 10–14)	Total	Total population of 10–18 year-olds
End 1932	55,365	28,691	19,244	4,656	107,956	
End 1933	568,288	1,130,521	243,750	349,482	2,292,041	7,529,000
End 1934	786,000	1,457,304	471,944	862,317	3,577,565	7,682,000
End 1935	829,361	1,498,209	569,599	1,046,134	3,943,303	8,172,000
End 1936	1,168,734	1,785,424	873,127	1,610,316	5,437,601	8,656,000
End 1937	1,237,078	1,884,883	1,035,804	1,722,190	5,879,955	9,060,000
End 1938	1,663,305	2,064,538	1,448,264	1,855,119	7,031,226	9,109,000
Beg. 1939	1,723,886	2,137,594	1,502,571	1,923,419	7,287,470	8,870,000

Abbreviations: HJ, Hitler-Jugend (Hitler Youth); DJ, Deutsches Jungvolk (German Young People); BDM, Bund Deutscher Mädel (League of German Girls); JM, Jungmädelbund (League of Young Girls).

During the later 1930s, when membership became compulsory, the attractions of the Hitler Youth began to wane. When everyone was forced to join there were some who did not care and were not interested. Discipline was tightened and there was a greater emphasis on drill. This upset many members. Then, during the war years, the number of leisure activities was cut. Playing fields and youth club buildings were bombed and many Youth leaders were called up for the war. Thousands of young Germans now created their own youth gangs and culture in opposition to the Hitler Youth.

SOURCE G

HER ZU UNS!

Hinein in die Hitler-Jugend

A poster urging young people to join the Hitler Youth.

Opposition to the Hitler Youth

There were three main groups of young people who opposed the Hitler Youth: the 'Edelweiss Pirates', the 'Meuten' and the 'Swing Movement'. The Pirates got together in parks or on street corners. Each group had about a dozen boys and a few girls. At weekends they would go on trips to the countryside and meet up with other Pirates. Hitler Youth patrols were often taunted and sometimes beaten up by the Pirates. Such incidents attracted the attention of the authorities; some members were warned first and the next time they were rounded up. Barthel Schink, a 16-year-old leader of the Cologne Pirates, was hanged in November 1944.

The Meuten were similar to the Pirates, mostly working-class and based in Leipzig. All in all, there were 1,500 of them in various gangs.

The Swing Movement was founded by young middle-class Germans who shunned German nationalist music and preferred instead to listen to jazz and swing. Swing clubs sprang up in Hamburg, Kiel, Berlin, Frankfurt and Dresden. Their dancing appalled the authorities, who banned live performances.

>> Activities

1 How does Source A illustrate Hitler's attitudes towards youth?

2 How were Sources B and C meant to indoctrinate young people?

3 How would you investigate the impact of anti-Semitic propaganda such as that shown in Sources B and C?

4 How far was the image of the Hitler Youth in Source G matched by the experiences of young Germans who did join the Hitler Youth?

5 What was the range of responses to the Nazi regime from young people?

Women and the family

'Kinder, Kirche und Küche' – Children, Church and Kitchen: this sums up the Nazi attitude towards women. The Nazis assumed that there was a 'natural' distinction between the sexes. Men were the productive and creative sex in the big world of politics and war. Women were reproductive, and essentially passive in the little world of the family home. This meant that women should stick to their 'natural' occupations as wives or mothers. If they had to work, they should choose occupations which reflected their 'natural' talents, such as nursing or social work, which would not endanger their ability to have children.

How successful were Nazi policies towards women and the family?

From 1936, girls had to join the Hitler Youth. At 14 they went from the League of Young Girls to the League of German Girls (BDM). Between 18 and 21 they could join the Faith and Beauty organisation and thereafter the National Socialist Organisation of Women (NSF). Some women saw a career in these groups and a means of avoiding the authority of their parents and families. Others valued membership because it helped them develop self-confidence and hold positions of leadership and responsibility.

SOURCE B

These population statistics were produced by historians. They cover the period 1929–39. After 1937, all the figures cover not only Germany but also Austria (invaded 1938) and the Sudetenland (invaded March 1939).

Year	Marriages	Live births	Deaths
1929	589,600		
1931		1,047,775	734,165
1932	516,793	993,126	707,642
1933	638,573	971,174	737,877
1934	740,165	1,198,350	724,758
1935	651,435	1,263,976	792,018
1936	609,631	1,277,052	795,203
1937	620,265	1,277,046	794,367
1938	645,062	1,348,534	799,220
1939	772,106	1,407,490	853,410

SOURCE A

Familienbildnis, *painted by Wolfgang Willrich in the 1930s. It shows the ideal Nazi family.*

Creating a 'racially pure' society

Nazi policy towards the family focused particularly on women because they were worried about the falling birthrate and the 'racial quality' of the population. The Nazis tried to tackle this problem in various different ways.

SOME MEASURES TAKEN TO IMPROVE THE BIRTH-RATE OF THE 'RACIALLY PURE' GERMAN PEOPLE:

> Some local authorities introduced rent, water or electricity rebates for large families.

> The Mother's Cross was awarded from 1938: gold for those with eight children; silver for those with six children; bronze for those with four children.

> The Law for the Reduction of Unemployment (June 1933) introduced interest-free loans of up to 1,000 Reichsmarks for young married couples on condition that the wife gave up work. Women were forbidden to act as judges or lawyers.

> The divorce laws were amended to make it easier to end 'unproductive' (i.e. childless) marriages.

Not all German mothers 'benefited' from these measures. Women who were socialist, pacifist, Sinti, Roma or Jewish were sterilised. So were men. 320,000 people suffered in this way between 1934 and 1939, men and women in equal numbers. In the three years 1934 to 1937, 80 men and 400 women actually died during these operations. For the 'racially useless', Nazi family policy meant not being allowed to have children.

SOURCE C

'You also belong to the Führer.' A propaganda poster aimed at German girls.

Nazi policy towards women and the war

Once war preparations started in 1937, the Nazis reversed their policies. Conscription and rearmament were gaining momentum and as they did so, a labour shortage developed. Having praised the virtues of motherhood and domesticity for so long, the Nazis now had to find ways to lure women back into jobs. Women were unimpressed. Dead-end, low-paid factory jobs were not attractive. Kindergarten provision and maternity leave made little impact. The number of women in paid employment only rose from 14.6 to 14.9 million between 1939 and 1944. This was not nearly enough to meet the demands of a wartime economy. Ironically, it was the government's emphasis upon the 'natural' roles of women in peacetime that produced undesirable consequences during wartime.

>> Activities

Use all the Sources and the background information.

1 What Nazi views of the family and of women are represented in the painting and the poster (Sources A and C)?

2 Study Source B. Between 1933 and 1939 how successful were the Nazis in

  a increasing the number of marriages?

  b increasing the number of births?

  Why do the statistics for the years after 1937 have to be used very carefully?

  In 1933 the population of Germany was 66,027,000. In 1937 it had reached 67,831,000. Is this evidence of success or failure for Nazi policies towards women and the family?

3 What evidence is there to suggest there were some contradictions in Nazi policies towards women and the family between 1933 and 1945?

A popular regime?

As you have seen, the Nazi regime was ruthless in its persecution of certain minority groups. But how was life under the Nazis for the majority of the German population?

Did most people in Germany benefit from Nazi rule?

The brief answer to this question is that it depends upon which period of Nazi rule you focus on, which particular group of Germans are being studied and how you define the term 'benefit'. Hitler was a popular leader with the majority of Germans until well into the Second World War. So, if his popularity is a litmus test, most Germans did consider they benefited from Nazi rule. But this does not mean that the Nazis were popular too. In this investigation you will study sources about groups of Germans who were not amongst the persecuted minorities.

Employment and the workers

Getting unemployment down was a priority for Hitler's government. The rearmament programme and conscription both took thousands off the unemployment register. The German Labour Front was set up to organise workers and direct them to jobs that needed doing. Public works such as afforestation projects, water conservation schemes and the building of houses, barracks and motorways got thousands of men back to work.

Once the Nazis were in power, Party membership shot up from 850,000 in 1933 to 2.5 million by 1935 and then to over 5 million at the outbreak of war in 1939. Party members were not just motivated by Nazi ideals. For many thousands of Nazi followers, their jobs, status and the necessities of life depended upon their commitment to the Party. Government organisations like the Labour Front were big employers too. By 1939 it was employing 44,500 paid officials. 'Jobs for the boys' benefited many Germans.

The economy and living standards

Not everyone benefited from Nazi interference in the economy and labour market, however. Small businessmen suffered because of the shortage of consumer goods which they sold for profit. They could not put their prices up to make up the shortfall because Nazi laws prevented them from so doing.

The Nazi regime also controlled food prices. In one way this was beneficial because there was no inflation. However, there were constant complaints about shortages of fats and about the poor quality of textiles and other goods which contained a high percentage of ersatz (substitute) materials in them. Wage rates were held down so workers did not experience an increase in their living standards. Since the destruction of their unions, they were in no position to bargain for improvements.

Leisure time

The Nazi organisation Strength through Joy (KDF) brought benefits to some people. It organised leisure activities for workers. Cheap holidays like cruises to the Canary Islands could be bought for just two weeks' wages. Although some workers did take advantage of this, places were mostly reserved for hardworking Nazi Party personnel.

People in the countryside

People in rural communities were pleased with benefits brought by the Labour Front, the Nazi organisations for women and young villagers, and the cheap holidays provided by KDF. Women benefited

SOURCE A

This graph shows the German unemployment figures for 1933–39.

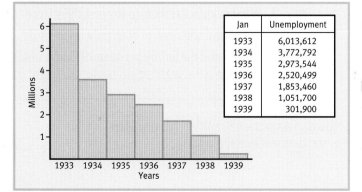

Jan	Unemployment
1933	6,013,612
1934	3,772,792
1935	2,973,544
1936	2,520,499
1937	1,853,460
1938	1,051,700
1939	301,900

Hurrah, die Butter ist alle!

Goering in seiner Hamburger Rede: „Erz hat stets ein Reich stark gemacht, Butter und Schmalz haben höchstens ein Volk fett gemacht".

'Hurrah, the butter is finished!' This picture by John Heartfield makes fun of a speech made by Hermann Goering when he said the choice for German people was 'guns or butter'.

Kraft durch Freude

Auch Du kannst jetzt reisen!

Besorge Dir noch heute eine Reisesparkarte der NSG „Kraft durch Freude". Der KdF-Wart Deines Betriebes und folgende Stellen geben sie kostenlos aus: Bank der Deutschen Arbeit, alle öffentlichen Sparkassen, Genossenschaftskassen (DGV und Raiffeisen), Thüringische Staatsbank.

A Strength through Joy poster, 1938.

particularly by being able to travel beyond the confines of the village. It brought them into contact with other women and allowed them to cross class boundaries. In many ways it actually liberated them from traditional village life. On the other hand, as war approached, demands on women increased. They were expected to combine the roles of mother, housewife and industrial worker.

Popular opinion in Nazi Germany

Hitler was popular. He had provided Germany with authoritarian leadership which is exactly what many Germans from all classes had wanted. He was successful in lowering unemployment and also in restoring German national honour through the Berlin Olympics in 1936, the re-occupation of the Rhineland in the same year, and the scrapping of the Versailles treaty. Instead of desperation and hopelessness, optimism and self-confidence reigned. All of this must have seemed a miracle to many Germans who had lived through the difficult times.

>> Activities

1 Did each of these groups benefit from Nazi rule: male workers; female workers; Nazi Party members; soldiers in the armed forces; small businessmen?

2 John Heartfield created Source B, which is a photomontage. He was a German Communist who left Germany in 1933 after the SA destroyed his work.

   a What point is Heartfield trying to make?

   b Is Source B of any value in investigating who benefited from Nazi rule?

   c Which groups of Germans would have shared Heartfield's attitude?

1939–45: Germany at war

In the years 1939–42 very little changed for most Germans. Many disliked being at war with England and France but Hitler's amazing military successes early on stifled some of the doubts people had about his policies. After 1942, the strains and stresses of running a war did have a profound impact on life in Germany. Who suffered and why during the war years?

How did the coming of war change life in Germany?

The effect of war on the German economy

Hitler knew that preparations for conflict had to be made and the German economy had been subject to a Four Year Plan between 1936 and 1940. In the early days of the war, the economy was little affected. The Nazis exploited the resources of the conquered territories: France paid Germany 1.75 billion Reichsmarks in 1940 and 5.55 billion in 1941, as well as being robbed of her raw materials. The German economy also benefited from foreign labour. By 1941, at the height of Nazi success in the war, just over 3 million foreign workers were labouring for the Germans.

However, as the tide of war turned against the Nazis, new pressures came to bear upon the German economy. Allied bombing raids were destroying factories and transport systems, and the running of the concentration camps in pursuit of the 'Final Solution' was draining resources away from the war effort. In spite of these problems, the Nazis succeeded in trebling armament production between 1942 and 1944. Once the Allied armies landed in Normandy in June 1944, however, and the Soviet armies rumbled towards Berlin, the Germany economy no longer had the resources of the occupied territories to fall back on. Shortages of fuel and food hit civilians hard and ever heavier air raids disrupted factory production.

SOURCE A

This table shows the number of bombs (in tons) dropped on Britain and Germany between 1940 and 1945.

	On Germany	On Britain
1940	10,000	36,844
1941	30,000	21,858
1942	40,000	3,260
1943	120,000	2,298
1944	650,000	9,151
1945	500,000	761

The effects of the Allied bombing raids

May 1943 saw the start of the heavy bombing of Germany by the British at night and the Americans by day. The results were devastating. In Hamburg, raids in July and August 1943 destroyed 60% of the city, wiped out 300,000 houses and killed between 60,000 and 100,000 people.

SOURCE B

This is taken from a diary by Mathilde Wolff-Monckeberg written in 1943. She was a housewife in Hamburg.

People here are curiously apathetic and dull. On their faces one can read despair, can sense wretchedness, irritation and exasperation wherever one happens to be: on the tram, in the post office, in the shops. Since the surrender of Stalingrad [January 1943] all is grey and still. Shop after shop has closed down, one tolerates discomforts, and forgets that life was ever different.

SOURCE C

'Black out! The enemy sees your lights.' A propaganda poster warning German civilians about British bombing raids.

The effects of terror bombing on morale are difficult to assess. The majority showed the usual signs of trauma: confusion, silence and blank gazes. A minority panicked; Germans were sometimes trampled to death in bunkers by other Germans. Some were able to master the situation and take appropriate action. Risking their lives, they fought flames to rescue those trapped in ruined buildings and defused unexploded bombs.

The effects of the war on German village life

Many rural communities had resisted outsiders, but from 1939 they had to accept evacuees and refugees from the bombings. Village populations rocketed but the available housing did not. Forced to share their homes and aware that they were losing the war, many villagers stopped supporting the Third Reich. From 1944 onwards some people openly defied Nazi officials by not declaring food they had produced. In a few cases villagers hid deserting soldiers.

Before 1939, agricultural work had been secure. Now people had to work in industry because of the demands of the war. The Nazis had promised to ensure the survival of rural German life; instead, they unleashed forces which effectively destroyed it.

Rationing

Morale on the home front depended on maintaining food supplies. The shortages at the end of the Great War had taught the Nazis that lesson. By and large Hitler's regime was successful in maintaining supplies; shortages never reached critical levels.

When war began, so did the rationing of items of daily diet. Ration-cards were distributed. In 1939 the meat ration was 700 grams per person per week; by 1945 it was 250 grams. During the winter of 1943 some Berliners enjoyed an unusual meat menu. Most of the city's zoo had been destroyed and many animals were killed. Berliners discovered that crocodile tail tasted like chicken if cooked long enough. Buffalo and antelope went down well and bear hams and sausages were much sought after. As ever in war, a black market flourished in food and items which were in short supply.

Evacuation

German parents sent their children out of the big cities to escape the Allied air raids. Austria and Bavaria were the main destinations. The Hitler Youth organised the evacuation programme and parents were encouraged to take up the offer with promises of a good education for their children. Many found separation from their families a terrible ordeal.

The Hitler Youth

Members of the Youth organisations found themselves doing all sorts of different jobs to help sustain the war effort on the domestic front. Boys helped the fire services, delivered post, distributed ration-cards and acted as guides during black-out. They also organised collections of metal, bones, kitchen waste, clothing and books.

Girls did their bit too. In kindergartens, old people's homes and hospitals they helped in whatever way they could. They brought coal and food for the homeless, war widows and refugees. They even formed choirs to entertain the sick and wounded.

SOURCE D

German refugees in the devastated centre of Berlin, 1945.

Women

The terrible human losses in the war and the labour shortage forced the Nazis to reverse their previous policy towards women. They tried to increase the birth-rate of Germans of 'pure stock' and tried to get women back to work. It was all to no avail. The incentives had little effect. Women's health was suffering. Indeed shortages of some foods, bombing raids, concerns over children's welfare, worries about loved ones at the front, and the disruption of the transport system all contributed to a serious deterioration of public health.

SOURCE E

This poster was designed to encourage women to work for the German railways during the war.

Resistance

During the war, opposition from youth groups grew stronger. News about concentration camps, about mass murder and the euthanasia programme leaked out and became widely known. In Berlin a group of young Jews led by Herbert Baum resorted to violence. They set fire to an anti-Soviet exhibition. The Gestapo arrested the whole group. Baum was tortured to death; the six others were beheaded on 18 August 1942. The families of those connected with the fire were immediately sent to Auschwitz, where they perished.

The 'White Rose' was a resistance group led by Hans and Sophie Scholl. Numbering about 15, they were mostly students at Munich University. On 18 February 1943 the Scholls were arrested while distributing leaflets encouraging young Germans to fight against the Nazi 'subhumans'. After three days' interrogation they were executed on 22 February 1943.

Hitler had opponents amongst upper-class Germans but they did not take any action until 1944 when they conspired to kill Hitler. They knew that they could get close to him by using their supporters in the German army. In July 1944, Claus von Stauffenberg, a senior army officer, left a bomb by a table in a conference room used by Hitler. The explosion killed four people but Hitler escaped serious injury. Those involved in the 'July Plot' were barbarically executed along with over 5,000 others connected with the conspirators.

>> Activities

Use all the Sources, the background information and your own knowledge.

1 How did the Allied air raids change people's morale from what it had been in the first few years of the war?

2 Compare the home front in Britain and in Germany. What were the similarities and differences in rationing and evacuation?

3 What changes did the war bring to the lives of

   a women

   b young people in Germany?

1933–45: Hitler's Germany

WHAT WAS IT LIKE LIVING IN HITLER'S GERMANY?

Hitler's rule over Germans depended upon coercion and consent. Most Germans went along with what Hitler was doing because they were satisfied with his leadership for various reasons.

> Hitler restored national pride by scrapping the hated Treaty of Versailles.

> He brought hope to many who desperately needed work.

> He represented strong, authoritarian government, which is what many Germans of all classes actually wanted.

> He dealt ruthlessly with minorities who were unpopular anyway.

WHAT WAS HITLER PLANNING TO ACHIEVE?

Hitler had three main aims:

> to create a national community of Germans;

> to deal with the 'Jewish problem';

> to launch a race war against the Soviet Union.

He deceived the German people by covering up his intentions about war until he was in control of Germany and his preparations were complete.

NAZI TERROR

Hitler used propaganda, terror and concentration camps to coerce Germans who were either not part of the Aryan 'master race' or who were political enemies.

> The Gestapo and the SS rounded up suspects, tortured them, and put them in camps.

> The Gestapo were helped by many ordinary German citizens who acted as snoopers and denouncers.

> Concentration camps were set up early in Hitler's rule in many parts of Germany.

> Minorities, especially Jews, were persecuted during the 1930s through laws intended to exclude them from German life. Many emigrated. After 1942, those that stayed were caught up in the Holocaust.

German civilians bury Jewish victims in Landsberg concentration camp, 1945. The atrocities committed in concentration camps were kept secret from German civilians. When Allied troops entered the camps they made local people bury the dead.

HOW DID PEOPLE REACT TO HITLER'S RULE?

> Many young people were happy to join the Hitler Youth to begin with as it provided opportunities for lots of outdoor activities. At school, children were indoctrinated with Nazi propaganda.

> Girls were taught to follow a role-model which centred around motherhood. For boys, the ideal was based upon the military life-style with drill, uniforms, rallies and weapons.

> Some Nazi Party members enjoyed the benefits of being an official. This brought status, perks and secure employment.

> Workers lost rights when their trade unions were destroyed, but gained employment in some of the public works projects initiated by Hitler.

> Rearming Germany's armed forces and conscription both helped reduce unemployment in preparing the country for war.

HOW DID WAR AFFECT THE GERMANS?

> The vast majority of Germans did not want war, but Hitler's initial successes set aside their doubts. After losing the battle of Stalingrad in 1943, however, the tide of war turned against Germany and Hitler's popularity dwindled.

> Life was hard for German soldiers and civilians. There was rationing, evacuation and some shortages though nothing as severe as in 1918.

> Nazi policy towards women was reversed as the labour shortage struck key industries. Incentives failed to persuade women to return to work. The birth-rate did not rise in response to the government's call to produce more soldiers.

> When Hitler committed suicide in 1945 his dream of a thousand-year-old Reich was left in ruins after just 12 terrible years.

The surviving leaders of Hitler's Third Reich were put on trial for war crimes at the Nuremberg law courts. Twelve received death sentences.

Germany since the end of the Nazi period

The Cold War

Fifty years ago the Second World War ended. Hitler and his Third Reich were no more and Nazi Germany was dust and ashes. The Allies (Britain, the United States and the Soviet Union) were friends during the war but disagreements soon broke out over what to do with the defeated Germany. The two new superpowers, the USA and the USSR, fell out and a new, 'cold' war began.

Germany became one of the main theatres of the Cold War as relations between the two new superpowers froze over. Germany and its pre-war capital, Berlin, mirrored the divisions in international relations between capitalist and communist countries; those who supported the USA and those who supported the USSR.

Recovery and reunification

During the 1950s and 1960s West Germany, supported by money from the USA, quickly recovered from the devastation of the war, while East Germany was left way behind, struggling under Communist rule. Relations between the

German people celebrate the reunification of Germany near the Brandenburg Arch.

two Germanies normalised during the 1970s and 1980s. Then, in 1985, Mikhail Gorbachev was appointed leader of the Soviet Union and the reforms he introduced in his own country were soon imitated in other parts of the Soviet empire like East Germany. In 1989 popular protest began — people clamoured for change. In November the Berlin Wall came down and a year later, in December 1990, the two Germanies were reunited.

Germany is once more at the centre of Europe. The country has a strong economy and its leaders shape many of the developments in the European Union.

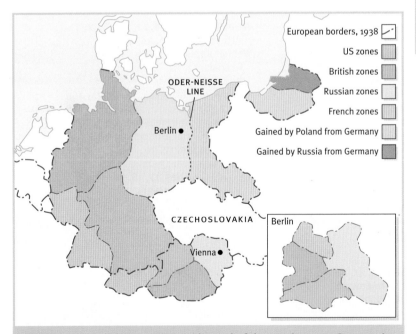

This map shows the situation at the end of the war in 1945. Germany's boundaries have been changed and the Allies occupy four zones of the country and of the capital, Berlin.

Index